An Educator's Guide to

Family Involvement in
Early Literacy

Author

Jennifer Prior, Ph.D.

SHELL EDUCATION

Publishing Credits

Dona Herweck Rice, *Editor-in-Chief*; Lee Aucoin, *Creative Director*;
Don Tran, *Print Production Manager*; Timothy J. Bradley, *Illustration Manager*;
Conni Medina, M.A.Ed., *Editorial Director*; Jamey Acosta, *Editor*;
Stephanie Reid, *Cover Designer*; Robin Erickson, *Interior Layout Designer*;
Corinne Burton, M.A.Ed., *Publisher*

Shell Education

5301 Oceanus Drive
Huntington Beach, CA 92649-1030
http://www.shelleducation.com
ISBN 978-1-4258-0753-5
© 2011 by Shell Educational Publishing, Inc.
Reprinted 2012

Table of Contents

Table of Contents (cont.)

What Is Family Involvement?

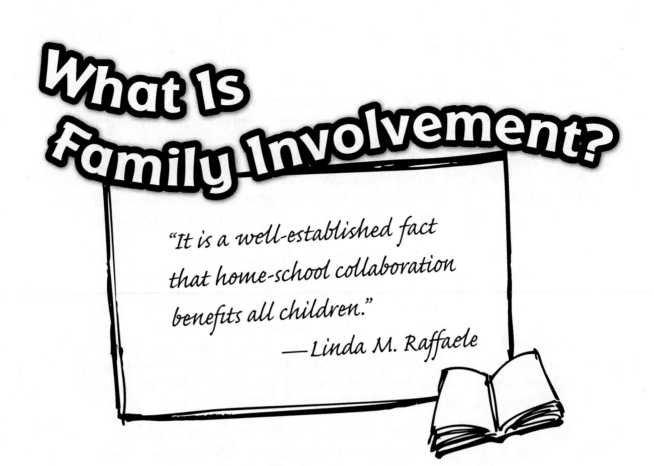

"It is a well-established fact that home-school collaboration benefits all children."

—Linda M. Raffaele

Introduction

Years ago, when I was preparing to be a teacher, I never thought about working with families. My dream was to work with children and that, I thought, would be the focus of my career as an early childhood educator. I was 21 at the time, and was too naive to realize that young children come with families and so, as their teachers, our job is to work with both. Most of us have heard the phrase, "A parent is a child's first teacher." How true this is! Children come to the classroom after years of interactions with family members in home environments that expose them to literacy in many ways, whether intentionally or unintentionally. It is our job as early childhood educators to tap into this wealth of knowledge that children gain before schooling in order to meet their needs in our classrooms.

A key element in this process, though, is to continue to involve families in their children's education. Families and teachers often feel that their jobs are vastly different. Teachers teach and parents parent. That's that. But really the roles of teacher and parent, although distinct, also overlap. When we partner with parents, we can work together to provide the best possible learning experiences for children.

Family involvement is much more complex than helping out in the classroom; it means developing and fostering effective partnerships between teachers and parents. This book will present family-involvement models and ideas to begin these partnerships. It will also focus on specific ways to get started with building parent-teacher partnerships and assisting parents with fun and interactive literacy activities at home. The book will provide ideas for effective parent-teacher communication, strategies for building partnerships, and ideas for parent involvement in the classroom. In addition, the book will provide plans for parent literacy workshops, literacy backpacks for parent-child home experiences, and informational literacy newsletters filled with ideas for parents and children. While the main focus will be on early childhood, ideas can be applied to students in the later elementary grades as well. The ideas and specific activities featured in this book are designed for instant use by classroom teachers with a teacher-friendly format.

Family involvement in education can take on many different forms. As teachers, we often first think that this refers to families coming to school and helping in the classroom or volunteering at schoolwide events. This is certainly a great way to involve families, and helping them to feel comfortable in the school environment is a positive endeavor. It is, however, important to remember that family involvement is much more than involvement at school.

Involvement at Home

First and foremost, family involvement should be encouraged at home. Showing interest, reading aloud, assisting with homework, and engaging in conversation about school and life are all ways to enhance the development of children's academic skills. Children whose families never set foot in the classroom but participate in such activities enjoy the academic benefits of family involvement more than those whose parents help in the classroom but do not participate in literacy activities in the home. By giving families ideas about how they can support their children's literacy learning at home, you help them provide these benefits for their children. Refer to the section on Literacy Experiences at Home (pages 33–102) for more information about the importance of family involvement.

Teacher-Family Partnerships

Another model for family involvement encourages partnerships that are established between families and teachers. With much involvement left in the hands of families, this is one area that we, as teachers, can actually work to achieve. As teachers, we can reach out to families and begin the necessary conversations to form valuable partnerships, allowing us to work with families as a team to assist children in their academic development. Refer to the section on Forming Teacher-Family Partnerships (pages 19–26) for more ideas.

Classroom-Based Involvement

Parent involvement in the classroom is probably the most familiar to teachers. In fact, when we think about how to get parents more involved, most of us think about how to get parents to come to school to help out. While classroom-based involvement is definitely encouraged, it is important to remember that all those wonderful benefits that come from parent involvement are more closely related to the kind of involvement that happens in the home. That said, creating an environment that is welcoming to parents and open for volunteerism is beneficial in that it allows the teacher the opportunity to make more contacts with those families who want to participate in classroom-based activities. This kind of involvement may include parent helpers during the regular school day or parents who help out with special events, such as seasonal parties or field trips. The most important thing to consider is parents' varying availability and providing different kinds of volunteer opportunities, as some parents may want to volunteer on a weekly basis, while others may want to help out a few times a year.

While family involvement can take on many forms, it is important to remember that the most important involvement is that which takes place at home. We can gently encourage families to participate in activities that contribute to their children's early literacy development by providing them with fun ideas that they can easily do at home. At the same time, we can continue to provide ways for parents to feel comfortable and assist in the school environment. In the next section, The Roots of Literacy, we will explore ways to begin forming partnerships with families. Refer to the section on Involving Families in School (pages 27–32) for a closer look at classroom-based involvement.

Benefits of Family Involvement

Early childhood education has gained a great deal of attention in recent years. As we examine the importance of these early years in school, we realize the importance of families and the role they play in their children's development and learning. A growing body of research has focused on the benefits of family involvement in early education. In particular, we can see the benefits to children when their families participate in literacy experiences with them. Let's take a look at what research says about the overall benefits to children when their families are involved in their education.

Carter (2002) explored the results of 70 studies about parent involvement. From these studies, the following common themes were found:

1. Parent involvement positively impacts student achievement at all levels of schooling.

2. When parents are involved in their children's education, their children typically do well in school.

3. When parents are involved during the early years of school, children make more successful transitions into classrooms. The children find the transition from home to school to be less traumatic.

4. When parents assist children with school projects at home, they positively reinforce and strengthen learning.

5. Mathematics and literacy skills improve when parents participate in the education experience.

6. Variations in student achievement exist in relation to culture, ethnicity, and socioeconomic backgrounds. When parents are involved with their children's education, this gap decreases.

Furthermore, Henderson and Berla (1994) state that income level and social status are not the best indicators of a child's achievement. Instead, they claim that achievement is linked more strongly to the following:

- a home environment that encourages learning

- expression of high expectations by parents

- parents' willingness to participate in their children's education, both in and outside of school

Benefits Related to Reading

Family involvement in education also has many benefits related to specific subject areas—particularly in reading.

A study of struggling first-grade readers (Faires, Nichols, and Rickelman 2000) provided parents with Reading Recovery training sessions. These sessions helped parents participate in reading lessons with their children. The study indicated that children of the participating parents experienced significant gains in reading assessments.

Children in second through eighth grade whose parents attended sessions about effective parent involvement exhibited greater achievement in reading and mathematics (Shaver and Walls 1998).

A Los Angeles study showed improvement of third graders' reading skills when parents participated in a program about parent-child communication, parenting, and learning activities for the home (Quigley 2000).

A study by West (2000) reported increased reading achievement for children whose parents read to them five minutes a day, three days a week.

Benefits Related to Early Childhood

Research makes a strong case for family involvement at all levels of children's education, but it is especially important during the early years. Research spanning the decades indicates the importance of such involvement with young children.

Goldberg (1989) reports that when parents get involved in their children's education early on, they are more likely to stay involved. In addition, Goldberg states that the long-term benefits to children as a result of sustained involvement is ultimately greater.

Kreider (2002) conducted a study of parents from low-income, ethnically diverse backgrounds. It was found that parents who were more involved in their children's education in the early years were more likely to visit the school and read to their children at home.

A longitudinal (ongoing) study of a program in Chicago indicated that parent involvement during preschool and kindergarten led to greater reading achievement, fewer grade retentions, and fewer special education placements (Miedel and Reynolds 1999).

Benefits to Families and Teachers

You are probably convinced by now that involving families in children's education is a good thing for children. In fact, you probably believed that even before you opened this book. But did you know that family involvement also has benefits for families and teachers? Faucette (2000) reports that family involvement benefits teachers in the following ways:

- improved morale
- higher teacher ratings by families
- increased support from families
- higher student achievement levels
- improved reputations in the informal community "grapevine"

When teachers encourage families to be involved in education at home and school, they report having a greater understanding of the cultures of their students' families. They also value parents' participation and recognize its importance with children (Epstein 2000).

Studies show that parents experience personal gains from this involvement as well. Early studies by Epstein (1983; 1984) show that when teachers are successful with involving families, families have a better understanding of what is going on in their children's classrooms and they feel more confident about the instructional abilities of the teachers. A personal responsibility is also commonly felt by parents to help their children with school-related projects at home, and they report having increased understanding of how to help their children in positive ways. Another benefit to parents is that their involvement in their children's education leads to increased confidence in parenting in general (Epstein 2000).

However, keep in mind that we want to encourage an appropriate balance of educational support in the home, so as not to cause undue stress on the child. Elkind (1990, 8) cautions:

> *"While the encouragement of early competence can have beneficial effects, say by enhancing self-esteem, it can have negative ones as well. The pressure for early competence is tied up with competition. And competition entails failure as well as success. Children are not always prepared to deal with the ups and downs of competition, and parents who urge their children to compete may not be sensitive to the frustrations and anxieties a child may suffer in the vagaries of competition. The demands on children for early competence thus confront them with the potential for an array of emotional problems that we in the helping professions must begin to recognize and respond to."*

While this should not hinder our efforts in encouraging family involvement, it serves as a reminder that the most successful family involvement focuses on encouraging a child's academic pursuits, valuing each child's educational process, and working together to support the whole child (Prior and Gerard 2007).

Where Do We Go From Here?

While reading, you may have been wondering how you are supposed to get families involved in their children's education. I asked myself this question over and over in those early years of my teaching career. I can hope families will want to participate, but can I really make that happen for the families of my students? The answer to that is "yes and no." You can not force parents to be involved, but you can certainly make it appealing and fun. And that is what the rest of this book is about.

As you continue to investigate the ideas presented in this book, you will learn more about the following:

- The roots of literacy and how much home environments have to offer children.

- The types of family involvement that are most effective.

- The specific ways you can establish partnerships with families.

- The various engaging and fun activities that families can do at home together.

Do you remember all of those benefits to teachers mentioned earlier in this section? Well, those benefits are yours for the taking simply by embarking on a journey of involving parents in their children's education.

Features of the Book

Take-home Letters—This book includes more than 30 letters (provided in English and Spanish). Each letter offers ideas for easy, fun, and engaging activities that families can do with their children to encourage literacy development at home. The letters are available on the Teacher Resource CD.

Teacher Resource CD—The Teacher Resource CD includes a variety of materials that support the content of this book. Below is an overview of the items included on the CD. For a detailed list of the contents of the CD, please see pages 159–160.

- English and Spanish versions of each letter (provided in pdf and Microsoft Word® format)
- templates for journal pages, thank-you cards, and reading charts
- bonus art images

The Roots of Literacy

"Children are made readers on the laps of their parents."

— Emilie Buchwald

Home-School Connection

As teachers, it is easy to approach family involvement from a deficit model, where families are viewed as the problem. From this perspective, teachers and schools know what is best, and they do what they can to get families to participate in the education process. Having this frame of mind actually serves as a hindrance to positive parent-teacher partnerships and must be avoided. Much of the foundation for early literacy is provided in the home environment and makes the child better prepared for school. So, it is important for us to recognize and value the experiences children have had at home and to let parents know we are grateful for what they have done in the years prior to schooling to prepare children for academic learning.

First we must recognize the benefits of home literacy environments as creating a foundation for children's literacy learning. There are studies that indicate that children's academic achievement correlates with supportive learning environments in the home (Clark 1984; Christenson 1995). These studies suggest that school-like qualities in the home help children to have smooth transitions between home and school, leading to school success. So, what about homes that do not reflect school-like qualities? Henderson and Berla (1994) state that the best indicators of a child's achievement include the following:

- Parents who create a home environment that encourages learning.

- Parents' expression of high educational expectations.

- Parents' interest in and willingness to participate in their children's education, both at school and in the community.

It is important, as teachers, that we acknowledge and value the home environments of all of our students as very likely being fertile grounds for literacy learning. A study by Purcell-Gates (1996) of 24 children from low-income families revealed that many of the families incorporated literacy activities in their daily lives. It was noted that parents and their children used written language throughout the day for a variety of purposes. Another study by van Steensel (2006) reported "evidence against the often-assumed one-to-one relation between socio-cultural factors and home literacy experiences, or, more specifically, against the assumption that low socioeconomic status and ethnic minority families fail to support children's literacy development" (378).

Literacy-Rich Environment at Home

Many families regularly read aloud to their children. This has been identified as an important practice that leads to later reading success. The U.S. Commission on Reading issued a statement that reading aloud to children is "the single most important activity in building the knowledge required for eventual success in reading" (Anderson et al. 1985, 23). In a study by Park (2008), it was determined that early home literacy activities, attitudes of parents toward reading, and the number of books at home impact children's reading performance. Park further states that "home literacy environments are important resources even for children from poor socioeconomic backgrounds to benefit from" (502). Research confirms these assertions, reporting that the number of books (including children's books) in the home is a predictor of achievement in school (Wobmann 2003; Foy and Mann 2003).

Teale (1984) describes homes that are considered "rich literacy environments" that very naturally include reading and writing activities. The children living in these homes interact positively with others who model involvement with literacy materials. The availability of reading materials in the home has proven to be a significant factor in early reading success (Morrow 1993). These homes often have library corners for children and a wide variety of books made available throughout the house.

Studies also report the significance of writing materials in the home. Children are encouraged to scribble and develop writing skills naturally, which enhances the reading process (Morrow 1993). Parents are responsive to their children's interest in literacy and provide literacy experiences and discussion. Therefore, children who bring more literacy knowledge with them to school ultimately perform better than those who do not (Yaden, Rowe, and MacGillivray 2000).

Link Between Literacy Development and Play

We know that children commonly play in the home environment, and research suggests a link between play and literacy development. Numerous studies in this area reveal that children incorporate literacy activities in play and that the presence of literacy materials encourages their use (Morrow and Rand 1991; Neuman and Roskos1990; Pellegrini et al. 1991). Children incorporate literacy behaviors, such as pretending to read a book to a doll or creating a grocery list, and learn about their functional uses. Roskos (2000) suggests that play acts as a "connector" to literacy, helping children build the mental structures needed to make meaning of print. Symbolic play also has a connection to the reading and writing abilities of young children. Bergen and Mauer (2000) conducted a study of 14 children from three different age groups, looking for the proportion of symbolic play and its relationship to the level of phonological awareness. The study revealed that children who engaged in more symbolic play (literacy-related and pretend) in the preschool years had higher levels of phonological awareness.

Providing Effective Learning Environments to Families

For the benefit of successful family involvement and the possibility of future parent-teacher partnerships, we must not assume that the home environments of our students do not support children's literacy development. Purcell-Gates (2000) encourages educators not to make such assumptions, in particular, about lower socioeconomic status families because, as her research suggests, socioeconomic status has little to do with underperformance in school. Van Steensel (2006) confirms this in his study, stating, "In the case of ethnic minority families, for example, we found that, although a number of them could indeed be characterized as being 'literacy-impoverished,' most families frequently engaged children in school-related literacy activities" (378). Van Steensel also reports that, from his interviews, he learned that parents responded to suggestions made to them about beneficial literacy activities and participated in shared reading, visits to the library, and singing with their children because they had heard these were valued practices.

As teachers, we should not only acknowledge the literacy support families provide for their children, but we should also assist them further by providing ideas for effective learning environments. We can help parents create realistic goals for their children. We can also welcome families into the school experience by expressing the value of their participation with their children's education at school and home. A sample letter with suggestions for fun and engaging literacy experiences at home is provided on pages 17–18 and on the Teacher Resource CD.

Encouraging Literacy Development at Home

Dear Family,

Did you know that children develop reading and writing skills through life experiences? Of course, this refers to reading books to your child, but it also refers to children's observations of the way you read and write at home.

Here are some things you can do at home to further enhance your child's reading and writing skills:

- Have a lot of books readily available.
- Set up a library corner in your home.
- Read books aloud to your child.
- Show interest in your child's activities (even those that do not involve literacy).
- Take frequent trips to the library.
- Talk to your child about books.
- Have fun with books by discussing and acting out stories.
- Provide writing materials such as paper, pencils, markers, and envelopes for your child to use.
- Model the way you create grocery or to-do lists.

Remember, your child is watching and learning from the literacy behaviors you engage in every day.

Sincerely,

_____

Fomentar el desarrollo de la lectoescritura en el hogar

Encouraging Literacy Development at Home

Querida familia:

¿Sabían que los niños desarrollan sus habilidades de la lectoescritura a través de las experiencias de la vida? Claro que esto no sólo se refiere a leer libros a su hijo, sino que también se refiere a las observaciones de los niños de la lectura y la escritura en el hogar.

Aquí están algunas cosas que ustedes pueden hacer para fomentar más el desarrollo de la lectoescritura con su hijo:

- Tener suficientes libros en su hogar.
- Disponer una biblioteca en un rincón en su hogar.
- Leerle libros en voz alta a su hijo.
- Hacer viajes frecuentes a la biblioteca.
- Hablar con su hijo sobre libros.
- Divertirse con los libros. Hablar del desarrollo de los cuentos que lean. Representar cuentos e historias.
- Actuar como modelo creando listas de compras o listas con las tareas pendientes.

Recuerden que su hijo está observando y aprendiendo de sus hábitos de lectura y escritura cada día.

Sinceramente,

_____

Forming Teacher-Family Partnerships

"Communication is the key to developing effective partnerships with parents."

—Kimberly B. Moore (2001)

Establishing Partnerships

When thinking about involving families in effective ways, it is important for us as teachers to rid ourselves of the "us versus them" mentality and, instead, think about forming partnerships. Children need both their families and their teachers to work together to bring about the best possible educational opportunities. Many of us are fearful of forming teacher-family relationships. We fear criticism. We fear making a mistake. I remember that during my first year of teaching I was petrified about working with families. Call me naive, but I never really thought about families. I just wanted to teach kids. Such is the case for many new teachers. "But when a teacher faces his or her fears and makes efforts to connect with parents, he or she will most likely find much more acceptance than criticism, more successes than mistakes, and more ways to connect than ever imagined" (Prior and Gerard 2007). Now, you may ask yourself, "How do I form partnerships with families?" Forming teacher-family partnerships involves a process, and it begins with planning for your first encounters.

Classroom Environment

First impressions are important when meeting families, so having a classroom environment that is cheerful and engaging is a great first step. The room should have open spaces, places to display children's projects, and be decorated appropriately, without a lot of clutter. "A cluttered, disorganized, or dismal classroom certainly does little to encourage communication between parents and teacher" (Swick 2003). When meeting parents for the first time, present yourself professionally and wear a smile that conveys warmth and a message that you're happy they are there.

The following are simple ways to engage and welcome families into the classroom:

- Greet family members at the door with a handshake and a smile.
- Give a tour of the classroom.
- Point out key features of the room, such as the writing center, library, and students' work on display.
- Provide resources for families to keep or borrow, such as books, informational papers, and educational games and puzzles.

Making Connections

Communication is the key to developing effective partnerships with parents, and there are many ways teachers can establish positive connections through communication (Moore 2002). The first thing you can do is send a letter to families letting them know who you are. Parents often have fears about leaving their children with a new teacher, so giving them some background information can be reassuring to them. While you want to maintain a professional role, this is a time when you can let parents see a personal side to your life. After reading this letter, you will likely find that family members comment about information you shared. Maybe they grew up near you or they have the same kind of dog. These small connections provide an opportunity for conversation and the beginnings of lasting partnerships. The letter provided below is just one example of content, style, and tone for your introductory letter. However, the letter you write reflects you, so you may prefer a more formal tone or to include more of your professional accomplishments. As you write your letter, keep in mind that it is important to project your enthusiasm and your overall interest in connecting with your students' families. Use the following questions to guide the letter you write:

- Where did you grow up?
- What are your hobbies?
- Who are your family members?
- What is an exciting experience you have had?
- What do you love about being a teacher?

Dear Families,

Welcome to Room 12! My name is Mark Wright and I would like to take a moment to tell you a little bit about myself. I have been a teacher for five years. My wife, Lina, and I have been married for nine years. We have three children: Makenna (6), Jack (4), and Bobby (3). My love for water keeps me at the beach and the pool even in stormy weather. My children share the same feeling and now play water polo and belong to the swim club. Our summer was busy, but productive. We vacationed and worked on many projects at home. Now I am ready for some fun learning, and I am looking forward to working with your child.

There is so much to do and learn this year. We have many fantastic activities and programs planned for your child.

I look forward to learning about each of you and getting to know your child. Please take a moment to write me a note, an email, or stop by the classroom to introduce yourself.

Many thanks!

Mr. Wright

Back-to-School Presentation

Each teacher has his or her own way of structuring the classroom and the school day, so it is important to share information about this with families in order for them to become familiar with the culture of your classroom. A back-to-school presentation can be a quick and effective way to let families know what they can expect. Before you create your presentation, think through the things you would like them to know. See below for examples of common topics:

- What are the classroom and/or school expectations?

- What are the school's behavior and grading policies? How are you implementing these policies in the classroom?

- What kinds of activities will their children experience this year?

- If you have centers, what is the purpose and role of each center?

- What does a typical day's schedule and routine look like?

- What are the extra activities that children will be involved in (e.g., P.E., art, library, music)?

- What is your philosophy for teaching young children?

- Where should children go when they arrive at school?

- What time does the school open with supervision for children? Are children permitted in the classrooms, halls, etc.?

- What is the routine at the end of the day? Where should children meet family members? What are the routines for children who take the bus?

- How can families participate in classroom activities? Will you have a sign-up sheet?

- Is it permissible for family members to drop in without an appointment?

- Are family members able to help out on projects from home?

- How should a family member contact you (e.g., email, note, phone message)?

Use this presentation as a means of setting families at ease and getting them (and their children) excited for the upcoming school year. Be sure to allow for questions after your presentation. You might want to suggest that questions pertaining to all families be asked during this time. Then have an appointment sheet available for any family members who have questions that pertain specifically to them or their child.

Phone Calls

One of the best ways to establish and maintain partnerships with families is to communicate with them on a regular basis. A great way to begin is to make a phone call home to each family within the first few weeks of school. Your phone call should not address any problems or issues related to the school's agenda. Simply convey to the parent how happy you are to have his or her child in your class and allow the parent to ask any questions he or she may have. This simple form of communication lets the parent know that you are willing to take that extra step to work together for the benefit of the child.

Weekly Newsletters

Weekly newsletters can be an extremely effective method of communication. Although it is a significant time commitment, it provides valuable information for parents and families. It is helpful to send out the newsletter on the first day of each week to tell families what is to come in the week ahead. Although it may be a bit daunting to commit to regular communication, parents appreciate knowing that they can expect to hear from you on a regular basis. The newsletter should be divided into sections that remain consistent throughout the year, so families know where to find information. Sections can include: announcements, information about what is to be taught, suggestions for homework, and even a section for listing donations for class projects. (See the sample newsletter on page 24.) You might even want to include questions that parents could ask their children about activities they did in class. For example, "Be sure to ask your child about the science experiment we're doing on Wednesday." This offers the parents a way to engage their child in conversation about their school activities.

Note: Many teachers have their own websites or use the school website to post important information for families. A website is great place to post your weekly newsletter, too.

Sample Weekly Newsletter

CLASS NEWS

Announcements

Don't forget to send in your permission slip for Friday's field trip.

Language Arts

This week we will read the book, *Cloudy with a Chance of Meatballs* by Judi Barrett. We will learn about tall tales and discuss the compound words featured in the book.

Your child will have the opportunity to write about daily weather.

Math

In Math, we will review what we learned last week about two-digit addition. The children will create their own problems for their classmates to solve.

Science/Social Studies

This week we will monitor the weather patterns in various places around the world.

Home Activities

Watch and discuss a weather report on TV with your child.

Read to your child 15 minutes daily.

Ask Your Child...

Ask your child about the guest speaker (weather man) who is visiting us on Thursday.

Donations

We will be making weather paintings next week using salt paint. If you have any salt you can donate, please send it with your child.

Have a great week!

Conferences

A few times a year, we have the opportunity to sit down with families one-on-one to discuss their children's progress in school. I don't know about you, but this was something that I would usually dread. While it was exciting to be able to report positive progress, it was also frightening to anticipate unexpected questions or sense frustration and hostility from family members. This is why the conference setting is so important in the process of forming positive partnerships with families. Here are a few tips to assist you as you plan for conferences.

Discussion Items and Setting

Create a comfortable environment for the conference. The setting should be free of distractions. To ensure a positive and productive conference, consider the following:

- If possible, provide adult-size chairs and a table for displaying student work.

- Plan ahead for the possibility of siblings attending the conference and set up an area (away, but within sight of the conference table) with books, coloring books, crayons, toys, etc.

- Begin each conference with positive comments about the child's academic and social progress.

- Have work samples, anecdotes of student activities, report cards and/ or printouts of mastered skills ready to share with family members.

- When appropriate, show work from earlier in the school year to compare with more recent work to show the child's progress.

- Address problems by offering possible solutions, and do not be afraid to ask families for their input about how to address these issues.

- Convey a sense of teacher-family partnership.

Ending the Conference

Communicate the importance of family involvement in the child's education. Ask if there is anything you can do to support the family in these endeavors at home. Make sure family members hear about the value they have in their child's academic development. You might also want to send the family home with a list of fun activities which they can do at home to support literacy development.

In the Classroom

One of the great benefits of family involvement is that parents often begin to feel more comfortable in the school environment and want to participate during the school day. Of course, if I heard someone say this 20 years ago, I would not have thought this to be a "great benefit." But the more I developed partnerships with families, the more I became comfortable with them in the classroom. Having family members assist in the classroom is a great way to have more adult guidance while, at the same time offering families the opportunity to get an inside peek at the learning environment that is so important to their children's development.

Getting Over Fears

Establishing partnerships with families can be very intimidating, but the fear won't go away by avoiding them. In fact, the more you reach out to develop partnerships with parents, the more your fears will be alleviated and the more likely you are to find support from the families of your students. It is definitely worth the initial fear to begin these positive relationships that will help further the educational development of the children in your class.

Involving Families at School

"Research shows that well-designed [family involvement] programs can boost academic achievement and even raise low-income students' test scores."

—Jones (2001)

Planning Your Strategy

As great as it is to have parents visit and help in the classroom, it can sometimes be a distraction and is certainly an added responsibility. What will you have them do? Will they be scrutinizing you when they are there? The best way to prepare for involvement in the classroom is to set boundaries and make plans. Let parents know from the beginning of the school year that they will have specific opportunities to help in the classroom. Define those jobs and set days and times when those jobs will be available.

If you teach at a school where parent involvement is scarce, you may be chuckling right now. You may find it difficult to get some families to show up for a conference, let alone help in the classroom. This was my experience for my first seven years of teaching, during which time I told parents they could show up at any time, unannounced, to just come whenever they could.

My last five years of teaching was the complete opposite. I had 20 or more parents each year who wanted to help in the classroom regularly. It was for this scenario that I needed to plan for helper jobs, including specific days and times when parents would come to the classroom. In some cases, I even had to have a rotating schedule with parents coming every other week to assist.

Do not be afraid to personalize the structure of your volunteer schedule to work best for you. For example, I never scheduled parents to come in on Mondays. I just needed the first day of the week to connect with the children and get the week's activities underway. I also did not schedule parents to come in during the first month of school. This was my time to establish a community with the children. Once we had a strong community and established routines, the doors were wide open for parents to volunteer. The point is that you need to create opportunities for families that fit with your personality and the community of your classroom.

Determining Parent Jobs

Take time to think through the ways you would want to involve parents in your classroom. Create descriptions of these roles and allow parents to sign up for them. This is a great way to begin the school year and communicate that you are thinking about them and the parts which they can play in the educational process. A sample sign-up sheet is provided on pages 30–31 and on the Teacher Resource CD.

When Family Members Arrive at the Classroom

Make preparations ahead of time for what families will do when they come to help in the classroom. If possible, make contact with family members. Greet them upon arrival. It is helpful to establish a routine with volunteers so that they know what to do each time they visit the classroom. For example, if volunteers arrive at a time when you are teaching, you might want to establish a location where they can find instructions for what they can do to get started.

Express Appreciation

While the school day can be hectic, try to grab an opportunity to express appreciation for the time the parent has donated to your class. Saying thank you, offering a smile, and sending periodic notes can go a long way to strengthen partnerships with parents. Refer to page 32 for sample thank-you cards. Reproducible thank-you card templates are provided on the Teacher Resource CD. You can reproduce and personalize your thank-you card for classroom volunteers.

How you involve parents in the classroom community is definitely a personal choice. So, take some time to think through the volunteer opportunities you would like to offer families in order to create an environment that is enjoyable to families and beneficial to the students.

Job Sign-Up

Dear Family,

We would love to have you help in the classroom this year. Take a look at the jobs listed below. Then indicate the ones that interest you.

Job Title: _____ Days/Times: _____

Job Description: _____

Job Title: _____ Days/Times: _____

Job Description: _____

Job Title: _____ Days/Times: _____

Job Description: _____

Job Title: _____ Days/Times: _____

Job Description: _____

Job Title: _____ Days/Times: _____

Job Description: _____

I would like to sign up for the following jobs. (List all that apply.)

_____

_____

Parent's name: _____

Child's name:_____

Phone number:_____

Email address:_____

Preferred method of contact: Phone or email (circle one)

Sincerely,

_____

BACK TO SCHOOL

Apuntarse para trabajar

Job Sign-Up

Querida familia:

Nos encantaría que se apuntaran para ayudar en el salón de clase este año. Miren los siguientes trabajos. Indiquen los que les interesen.

Puesto: _____ Días/Horas: _____

Descripción del trabajo: _____

Puesto: _____ Días/Horas: _____

Descripción del trabajo: _____

Puesto: _____ Días/Horas: _____

Descripción del trabajo: _____

Puesto: _____ Días/Horas: _____

Descripción del trabajo: _____

Puesto: _____ Días/Horas: _____

Descripción del trabajo: _____

Me gustaría apuntarme para ayudar haciendo los siguientes trabajos. (Enumeren todos los que apliquen.)

_____

_____

Nombre del padre: _____

Nombre del niño: _____

Número de teléfono: _____

Correo electrónico: _____

Método preferido para contactarles: Número de teléfono o correo electrónico (marque uno con un círculo)

Sinceramente,

_____

BACK To School

Sample Thank-You Cards

#50753—An Educator's Guide to Family Involvement in Early Literacy

Literacy Experiences at Home

"Books, to the reading child, are so much more than books—they are dreams and knowledge, they are a future, and a past."

—Esther Meynell

Bringing Literacy Home with Fun Activities

This part of the book will provide you with a variety of activities for families to do at home in order to enhance their children's literacy. The following section provides ideas for families in the following areas:

- Read-Aloud Activities
- Environmental Print Activities
- Literacy Backpacks
- Literacy Newsletters

Read-Aloud Fun

According to studies by the National Institute of Child Health and Human Development (NICHD 2000), there are interventions that are shown to be precursors for development of literacy skills. Two of the five identified interventions are shared reading experiences and parent programs. Shared reading refers to the practice of reading aloud to a child. It involves adult-child interaction and discussion during read-aloud experiences. Parent programs were described as providing techniques to parents that they can use with their children. The importance of reading aloud to children is further emphasized by the Center for the Improvement of Early Reading Achievement (CIERA 2001b), which states that students should be read to aloud daily and that teachers should "encourage parents or other family members to read aloud to their children at home" (22). In its document, *Put Reading First: Helping Your Child Learn to Read*, CIERA recommends that parents provide opportunities for children to "listen and respond to stories read aloud" (2001b, 2).

Finger Puppets, Paper-Bag Puppets, and Dramatizing Stories

Taking the time to get to know each of the main characters in a story is a key step in building comprehension skills. After reading a story aloud one time, families can discuss the characters. Then using a puppet activity or dramatic play, children can bring the characters to life, re-enact the story, and engage in a fun literacy-building activity. Sample letters for these activities are provided on pages 35–40 and on the Teacher Resource CD.

Asking Questions

It is important for children to engage in and interact with the stories that they read and hear. Families can do this by implementing simple questioning strategies when reading aloud to their children. Many families probably do this naturally as they discuss the books they read with their children. A sample letter for this type of activity is provided on pages 41–42 and on the Teacher Resource CD.

Finger Puppets

Dear Family,

Reading aloud to your child is not only beneficial for literacy development, but it is also great fun. Make and use finger puppets to extend the story reading. After reading a story to your child, discuss the main characters. Then work with your child to draw and color each character's face and body on a finger-puppet outline below. Cut out the outlines and tape together where indicated. Then reenact the story together, using the puppets.

Sincerely,

_____

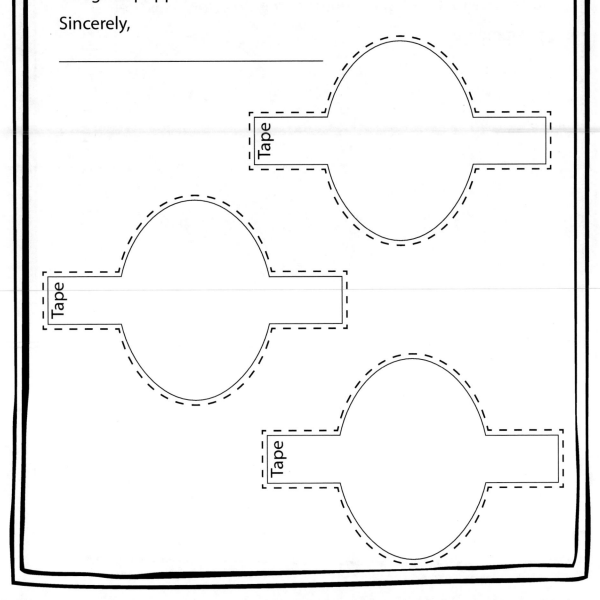

Títeres de dedo

Finger Puppets

Querida familia:

Leerle en voz alta a su hijo no sólo es beneficioso al desarrollo de la lectoescritura, sino también es bastante divertido. Aquí está una manera para extender la lectura de cuentos al crear títeres de dedo. Después de leerle un cuento a su hijo, hablen sobre los personajes principales. Luego trabajen con su hijo para colorear la cara y el cuerpo de cada personaje en la silueta del títere de abajo. Recorten la silueta y peguen con cinta adhesiva donde se indica. Luego representen juntos el cuento usando los títeres.

Sinceramente,

_____

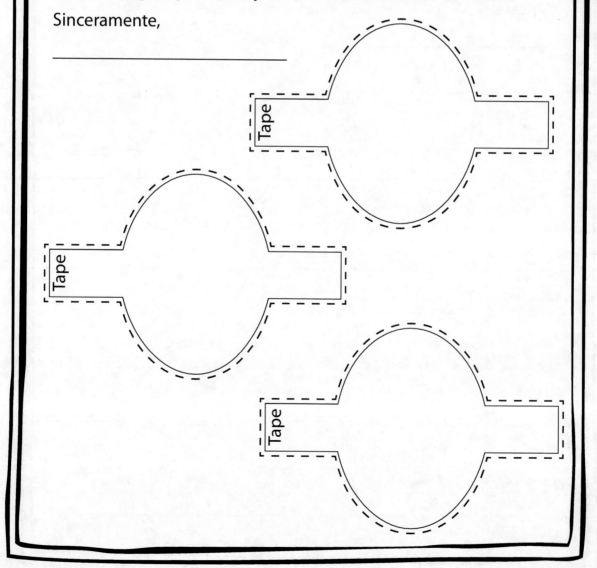

Paper-Bag Puppets

Dear Family,

After reading a book aloud to your child, review the story events using paper-bag puppets. To make a puppet, you will need:

- a paper bag
- crayons or markers
- construction paper *(optional)*
- glue *(optional)*
- scissors *(optional)*

Place your hand inside the folded bag, curving your fingertips over the flap at the base of the bag. By moving your fingers up and down, you can see where the puppet's mouth will be. Now color facial features on the bag. If desired, cut out and glue on construction-paper accessories.

Have fun!

_____

Títeres hechos de bolsas de papel

Paper-Bag Puppets

Querida familia:

Después de leerle en voz alta un libro a su hijo, diviértanse repasando los eventos del cuento usando títeres hechos de bolsas de papel. Para hacer un títere, necesitarán:

- Una bolsa de papel
- Crayones o marcadores
- Opcional: cartulina, pegamento, tijeras

Coloque su mano dentro de la bolsa doblada, curvando las puntas de los dedos sobre la solapa de la base de la bolsa. Al mover sus dedos hacia arriba y hacia abajo, podrán ver dónde quedará la boca del títere. Ahora coloreen rasgos de la cara en la bolsa. Si desean, recorten y peguen adornos con la cartulina.

¡Que se diviertan!

_____

Dramatizing Stories

Dear Family,

A fun way to follow up the reading of a story is to act it out with your child. Talk about two of the characters from the story. Discuss their personalities and the things that happened to them. Then select roles and act out the story together. If desired, create costumes using simple materials, such as blankets, pillowcases, and aprons.

Re-create the Setting

After reading a book to your child, draw your child's attention to the setting of the story. Was the setting realistic? Was it make-believe? Work with your child to re-create the setting in one of a variety of ways. See below for suggestions:

1. Draw a picture of the setting.

2. Use clay or salt dough (see recipe below) to create different objects in the story's setting.

3. Create a finger painting of the setting.

4. Pour a layer of salt or flour in the bottom of a cake pan. Use your finger to draw objects from the story.

Salt Dough Recipe

Ingredients: 1 cup of flour

½ cup of salt

1 cup of water

Mix ingredients together to make a pliable dough. Add more flour or water, if necessary, to create desired consistency.

Sincerely,

_____

Dramatizar los cuentos

Dramatizing Stories

Querida familia:

Una manera divertida para continuar con la lectura de un cuento es representarlo con su hijo. Hablen sobre dos de los personajes en el cuento. Hablen sobre sus personalidades y las cosas que les ocurrieron en el cuento. Luego seleccionen papeles y representen el cuento juntos. Si desean, crean disfraces con materiales sencillos como cobijas, fundas y mandiles.

Recrear el escenario

Después de leerle un libro a su hijo, puntualicen el escenario del cuento. ¿El escenario fue realista? ¿Fue imaginario? Trabajen con su hijo para recrear el escenario en una de una variedad de modos. Vea abajo para sugerencias:

1. Haga un dibujo del escenario.

2. Use arcilla o masa (vea la receta siguiente) para crear diferentes objetos en el escenario del cuento.

3. Crea una pintura del escenario hecha con los dedos.

4. Vierta una capa de sal o harina en el fondo de un molde de pastel. Use el dedo para dibujar objetos del cuento.

Receta de masa salada

Ingredientes: 1 taza de harina

½ taza de sal

1 taza de agua

Mezcle los ingredientes para crear masa moldeable. Agregue más harina o agua, si es necesario, para conseguir la consistencia deseada.

Sinceramente,

_____

Asking Questions

Dear Family,

When reading aloud to your child, it is important to interact with the story. You can do this before, during, and after the reading by asking questions. Try some of these questioning strategies with your child.

Before Reading

Look at the cover of the book. Ask your child questions about what he or she sees, such as:

- Where do you think the story takes place?
- What things do you recognize?
- What do you think the story will be about?

During Reading

Asking questions during the story helps your child to interact with the text, but don't ask so many questions that it detracts from the story. Every so often, ask questions such as:

- What do you think will happen next?
- What would you do if that happened to you?
- How do you think (the character) feels?
- What do you see in the illustration?

After Reading

Take a few minutes to reflect on the story by asking questions such as:

- What was your favorite part of the story?
- Did you like how the story ended?
- What other adventures do you think the main character will have?

Sincerely,

_____

Hacer preguntas

Asking Questions

Querida familia:

Cuando le lean en voz a alta a su hijo, es importante interactuar con el cuento. Pueden conseguir esto al hacer preguntas antes, durante, y después de la lectura. Traten de usar algunas de estas estrategias de preguntas con su hijo.

Antes de la lectura

Observen la portada del libro. Háganle preguntas a su hijo acerca de lo que él o ella vea, tales como:

- ¿Dónde crees que toma lugar este cuento?
- ¿Qué cosas reconoces?
- ¿De qué piensas que se tratará el cuento?

Durante la lectura

Hacer preguntas durante el cuento le ayuda a su hijo a interactuar con el texto, pero no deberían hacer tantas preguntas que le resta valor al cuento. De vez en cuando, hagan preguntas, tales como:

- ¿Qué piensas que sucederá luego?
- ¿Qué harías si eso te pasara a ti?
- ¿Cómo piensas que (el personaje) se siente?
- ¿Qué ves en la ilustración?

Después de la lectura

Tomen unos minutos para reflexionar sobre el cuento al hacer preguntas, tales como:

- ¿Cuál fue tu parte favorita del cuento?
- ¿Te gustó cómo terminó el cuento?
- ¿Qué otras aventuras piensas que tendrá el personaje principal?

Sinceramente,

_____

Environmental Print Activities

"Reading was the most valuable gift I ever received. When I would become lonely for my mother, I would read the labels in my grandmother's store. I would be carried off to the faraway places on the labels."—Maya Angelou (in an interview with Oprah Winfrey), July 2003

While people often think that literacy development begins when children start school, most educators understand that children are aware of and can read print in their surroundings. Children as young as age two can recognize hundreds of words in the environment (Anderson and Markle 1985). Environmental print—print in a child's surroundings and community—consists of logos, road signs, product labels, store signs, and billboards. Children learn that this print is functional and meaningful. Young children have a natural interest in environmental print materials, so parents can build on this by pointing out familiar print and placing empty product packaging in play areas (Prior and Gerard 2004).

So, what does the research say about how much environmental print impacts literacy development? There has been a debate over the years about environmental print and whether children's exposure to it really does assist in the process of learning to read (Christie, Enz, and Vukelich 2002; Christie et al. 2003; Harste, Burke, and Woodward 1982; Kuby and Aldridge 1997; Prior 2003). While children often have difficulty recognizing environmental print words when color and graphics are removed, there are some factors that help children to recognize environmental print words in decontextualized forms. According to Prior and Gerard (2004), the adult plays a key role in helping the child transfer from recognition of print in the environment to the process of reading. "When an adult draws attention to the letters and sounds in environmental print words, children are more likely to transfer this knowledge to decontextualized print—text without color and graphics" (25). For this reason, it is important to make parents aware of the benefits of drawing their children's attention to environmental print in the home. Pages 44–55 provide sample letters for fun activities you can offer families for using environmental print in creative and entertaining ways at home. The letters offer easy-to-use ideas to families for environmental print games which they can make and enjoy with their children. The letters are also provided on the Teacher Resource CD.

Environmental Print Activities

Dear Family,

Environmental print refers to the print, signs, logos, and labels that your child recognizes in your home and community. By pointing out this familiar print, and drawing your child's attention to the letters and sounds in the text, your child will begin to recognize that print is meaningful and that it is made up of individual letters and sounds. Try some of these activities at home.

Playing with Real Objects

Adding real-life environmental print items to the play area encourages children to behave as readers and writers while they use the items in play scenarios. Provide your child with empty cereal boxes, restaurant bags, or pizza boxes to use as they play. You can also provide cookbooks and writing materials for children to use. You'll notice that your child will use such items as he or she observes their use in the home.

Cereal Box Puzzles

Don't throw away an empty cereal box; instead, use it for literacy play. Simply cut off the front panel of the box and cut it into puzzle pieces. (For younger children, cut the panel into five to seven pieces. For older children, cut it into 10 to 15 pieces.) Then encourage your child to solve the puzzle. You'll notice that your child will likely pay attention to letters on the box as well as the pictures to help with puzzle assembly. Any cereal box that is familiar to your child can become a fun, literacy-enhancing puzzle!

Happy playing!

_____

Grocery Delivery

Actividades relacionado a los impresos del ambiente

Environmental Print Activities

Querida familia:

Los impresos del ambiente se refieren a las letras, carteles, logotipos y etiquetas que su hijo reconoce en su hogar y la comunidad. Al hacerle notar a su hijo las letras y los sonidos en el texto, su hijo empezará a reconocer que las cosas impresas son importantes y que se componen de letras y sonidos individuales. Intenten algunas de estas actividades en casa.

Jugar con objetos reales

Llenar las áreas de juego con objetos impresos reales anima a los niños a comportarse cómo lectores y escritores cuando los usen en los juegos. Proporcionenle a su hijo cajas de cereal vacías, bolsas de restaurantes, cajas de pizza o cajas de curitas para usar mientras juegan. También pueden proporcionar libros de cocina y materiales para la escritura para que los niños los usen. Notarán que su hijo usará tales objetos conforme él o ella observe cómo se usan en su hogar.

Rompecabezas con cajas de cereal

No echen una caja de cereal vacía a la basura, más bien úsenla para hacer un juego de lectoescritura. Simplemente recorten el panel delantero de la caja y recorten pedazos para hacer un rompecabezas. (Para los niños pequeños, recorte el panel en 5 a 7 pedazos. Para los niños mayores, recórtelo en 10 a 15 pedazos.) Luego animen a su hijo a resolver el rompecabezas. Ustedes notarán que su hijo probablemente le preste atención a las letras en la caja además de los dibujos cuando ayude a armar el rompecabezas. ¡Cualquier caja de cereal que su hijo reconozca puede llegar a ser un rompecabezas divertido que fomente la lectoescritura!

¡Que se diviertan jugando!

Grocery Delivery

Interact with Environmental Print

Dear Family,

Print is all around us. It helps your child to understand that text is meaningful. Try some of these activities to encourage your child's interaction with print.

Food Folder

Allow your child to collect the logos from favorite food packaging. Then glue these logos inside a file folder or a sheet of paper that is folded in half. Encourage your child to "read" the logo names and talk about his or her favorite foods.

Grocery Store Field Trips

At the grocery store, ask your child to point out items that he or she recognizes and to identify letters recognized in the logos.

Concentration!

Create a fun memory game with logos from familiar items in the home. Gather two each of 10 different logos. For example, you may choose logos such as Cheerios®, Burger King®, or Legos®. Glue each logo to an index card. Then turn all of the cards facedown. The child turns over two cards at a time and tries to find a match. If the cards selected don't match, turn them facedown and try again. You can increase the difficulty of this game by having the child match a logo to its beginning letter. So, half the cards would have logos on them and the other half would have corresponding beginning letters on them.

Sincerely,

_____

Interactuar con impresos del ambiente

Interact with Environmental Print

Querida familia:

Hay impresos a todo nuestro alrededor. Ayudan a que su hijo entienda que el texto es significativo. Intenten algunas de estas actividades para animar a su hijo a interactuar con impresos.

Carpeta de comida

Dejen que su hijo coleccione logotipos de cajas de una de sus comidas favoritas. Luego peguen estos logotipos dentro de una carpeta con archivos o en una hoja de papel que se doble a la mitad. Animen a su hijo a "leer" los nombres del logotipo y a hablar sobre sus comidas favoritas.

Viajes de recreo al supermercado

Pídanle a su hijo que señale objetos de comida que él o ella reconozca. Hasta pueden pedirle a su hijo que identifique letras que reconozca en los logotipos.

¡Concentración!

Crean un juego divertido que pruebe la memoria con logotipos de objetos familiares en el hogar. Junten dos de 10 distintos logotipos. Por ejemplo, pueden elegir logotipos como Cheerios®, Burger King®, Legos®, etc. Peguen cada logotipo en una tarjeta de índice o en un cuadro de cartulina. Luego volteen todas las tarjetas para que estén boca abajo. El niño debe voltear dos cartas a la vez buscando un par. Si las tarjetas que se seleccionan no hacen par, voltéenlas para que queden boca abajo e intenten de nuevo. Pueden aumentar la dificultad de este juego al hacer que el niño empareje un logotipo a su letra inicial. Así que la mitad de las tarjetas tendría logotipos pegados en ellas y la otra mitad tendría las letras iniciales correspondientes en ellas.

Sinceramente,

_____

Environmental Print at Home

Dear Family,

It's really very simple to have your child interact with print in the environment. Your child sees familiar print in your home every day. Try some of these activities for fun with print.

Cereal Book Reading

Create a book out of empty cereal boxes. Cut the front panel off each empty cereal box that is recognizable to your child. When you have collected an assortment of panels, stack the box panels and use a three-hole-punch to punch holes along the left side. Then bind the panels together with string, yarn, or metal rings. Your child will enjoy turning the pages and "reading" the cereal box pages.

Coupon Sorting

Cut out coupons for a variety of products that are familiar to your child. Then play a sorting game. Coupons can be sorted in the following categories:

- Things I like/Things I don't like
- Things to drink/Things to eat
- Things that are healthy/Things that are unhealthy
- Things we eat/Things we don't eat

Read the Pantry

Provide your child with a pointer of some kind (e.g., a ruler, a wooden spoon). Then have your child point to and read the items in the pantry that he or she recognizes. For an added challenge, ask your child to identify the letters in the words.

Sincerely,

_____

Impresos del ambiente en casa

Environmental Print at Home

Querida familia:

Es muy sencillo hacer que su hijo interactúe con impresos en su ambiente. Su hijo ve impresos familiares en su casa cada día. Pruebe algunas de estas actividades divertidas con los impresos.

Lecturas de libros de cereal

Crean un libro usando cajas de cereal vacías. Recorten el panel delantero de cada caja de cereal vacía que le sea familiar a su hijo. Cuando hayan coleccionado varios, apilen los paneles de las cajas y perforen tres hoyos al lado izquierdo de cada uno. Luego junten los paneles con hilo, cuerda o anillos de metal. Su hijo disfrutará pasándose las páginas y "leyendo" las páginas de la caja de cereal.

Clasificar los cupones

Recorten cupones de una variedad de productos que le sean familiares a su hijo. Luego jueguen a clasificar los cupones. Los cupones se pueden clasificar en las siguientes categorías:

- Cosas que me gustan/Cosas que no me gustan
- Cosas para tomar/Cosas para comer
- Cosas saludables/Cosas no saludables
- Cosas que comemos/Cosas que no comemos

Lean la despensa

Proporcionenle a su hijo algo que pueda usar para señalar (una regla, una cuchara de madera, etc.). Luego revisen su armario de cocina o despensa y hagan que su hijo señale y lea los objetos que reconozca. Como un reto adicional, pidanle a su hijo que les diga las letras que reconoció en las palabras.

Sinceramente,

_____

Fun with Environmental Print

Dear Family,

The following activities will help your children to recognize that print is meaningful and that there is a purpose for reading.

I Spy in the Pantry

Open the pantry or food cabinet and play a fun literacy game. Provide your child with clues about an item you see there. For example, you might say:

Question: *I spy something that is crunchy and orange. Its name begins with a G. I wonder if it can swim.*

Answer: *Goldfish® crackers*

Alphabet Book

Create an alphabet book with your child. Staple together a 26-page booklet and a cover. Label the top of each page with a different letter of the alphabet. Then have your child collect product packaging from around the house. Familiar logo cutouts can be glued onto the corresponding pages of the booklet. Continue adding logos to the booklet, creating a letter collage on each page.

Go Fish!

Make a game of Go Fish! with familiar print logos. Collect two logos each for a variety of items. Glue each logo to a different index card or a construction-paper square. The object of the game is to match logos. Deal four cards to each player and stack the remaining cards facedown. The first player then asks a question such as, "Do you have any Q-Tips®?" If another player has a card with a Q-Tip® logo, he or she gives away the card and draws one from the pile. The player with a match lays down the matching cards. If another player does not have the requested logo, the player draws a card from the pile. The first one to create matches with all their cards is the winner.

Happy playing!

Divertirse con impresos del ambiente

Fun with Environmental Print

Querida familia:

Las siguientes actividades ayudarán a su hijo a reconocer que el texto en los impresos tiene importancia y que hay un propósito para leer.

Yo espío en la despensa

Abran la despensa o el armario de la cocina y jueguen un juego divertido que fomente la lectoescritura. Proporcionenle a su hijo pistas sobre un objeto que ustedes vean. Por ejemplo, podrían decir:

Pista: Yo espío algo que es crujiente y anaranjado. Su nombre empieza con una G. Me pregunto si ellos pueden nadar.

Respuesta: Galletas de *Goldfish®*

Libro del alfabeto

Crean un libro del alfabeto con su hijo. Engrapen un librito de 26 páginas y una portada. Etiqueten cada página con una letra distinta del alfabeto. Luego hagan que su hijo coleccione empaques o cajas de productos en la casa. Peguen recortes de logotipos familiares en las páginas correspondientes del librito. Sigan agregando logotipos al librito, creando un collage de letras en cada página.

¡Vete a pescar! (Go Fish)

Hagan un juego de ¡Vete a pescar! con logotipos impresos familiares. Coleccionen dos del mismo logotipo para tener una variedad de productos. Peguen cada logotipo en una tarjeta de índice diferente o en un cuadro de cartulina. El objetivo del juego es emparejar logotipos. Repartan cuatro tarjetas a cada jugador y apilen las tarjetas que queden boca abajo. El primer jugador pregunta, por ejemplo, —¿Tienes Q-Tips®?— Si otro jugador tiene una tarjeta con un logotipo de Q-Tips®, le da a ese jugador la tarjeta y saca una de la pila. El jugador con un par retira las tarjetas del par. Si otro jugador no tiene el logotipo pedido, el jugador saca una tarjeta de la pila. El primer jugador que crea pares con más tarjetas es el ganador.

¡Que se diviertan!,

_____

Environmental Print Is Everywhere

Dear Family,

Here are some more activities that you can do with your child to help him or her take notice of print in your home and community.

Take a Drive

When driving through your community, point out signs of familiar locations, such as the grocery store, a gas station, or a bookstore. You can even play a game where you and your child look for all of the signs you can find that contain a particular letter. Ask your child to identify the sound that the letter makes and emphasize that sound when pronouncing the word.

Street Signs

Your child likely recognizes many street signs in your community. While out for a walk or while driving through town, have your child identify familiar words on signs. Be sure to point out stop signs, yield signs, railroad-crossing signs, hospital signs, and names of streets.

Healthy and Clean

Have a discussion with your child about the kinds of things we do and the kinds of products we use in order to stay healthy. For example, talk about why we brush our teeth, take baths, and wash our clothes. Then, with your child, collect logos from items that help him or her to stay healthy and clean, such as logos from toothpaste, shampoo, soap, or children's vitamins. Make a poster of the items that help your family to stay healthy and clean.

Sincerely,

_____

EXIT

Los impresos del ambiente están en todas partes

Environmental Print Is Everywhere

Querida familia:

Aquí hay más actividades que ustedes pueden hacer con su hijo para ayudarle a fijarse en los impresos en su hogar y en la comunidad.

Den un paseo

Cuando conduzcan por la comunidad, señale los letreros de locales familiares como el almacén, una gasolinera, una librería, etc. Inclusive pueden jugar un juego en el que ustedes y su hijo buscan tantos letreros como puedan encontrar que contengan cierta letra. Pídanle a su hijo que identifique el sonido que esa letra hace y destaquen ese sonido cuando pronuncien la palabra.

Letreros de la calle

Su hijo probablemente reconoce muchos letreros de la calle en su comunidad. Mientras caminan o conducen por la comunidad, haga que su hijo identifique palabras familiares en los letreros. Asegúrense de señalarle señalamientos de Alto, señalamientos de Ceda el paso, señalamientos de Cruce de ferrocarril, letreros de hospitales y los nombres de las calles.

Saludable y limpio

Tengan una conversación con su hijo acerca de los tipos de cosas que hacemos y los tipos de productos que usamos para mantenernos saludables. Por ejemplo, hablen sobre por qué nos cepillamos los dientes, nos bañamos y lavamos nuestra ropa. Luego coleccionen junto con su hijo logotipos de cosas que nos ayudan a mantenernos saludables y limpios como la pasta de dientes, el champú, el jabón, las vitaminas para niños, etc. Hagan un letrero de las cosas que ayudan a todos en su familia a mantenerse saludables y limpios.

Sinceramente,

_____

EXIT

Environmental Print and Literacy

Dear Family,

Studies show that when children interact with print in the environment, it benefits their literacy development. You can draw your child's attention to print in your home and in the neighborhood. You can also mention the letters at the beginnings of words and tell your child the sounds that those letters represent. By drawing your child's attention to the letters and sounds in the environment, you are helping him or her to recognize that print is everywhere! Try some of the following activities for more fun with environmental print.

Logo Stories

Encourage your child to collect the logos from favorite toys, foods, stores, etc. and place them in an envelope. On occasion, sit down with your child and have him or her select one of the logos. Glue the logo on a sheet of paper and ask your child to tell a story about it. Write the story below the logo while your child dictates. Collect the stories and assemble them into a booklet.

Letter Hunt

Play a game in your house where you and your child search for all the letters that you can find. Encourage your child to look at letters that might be on the walls, on the refrigerator, inside the refrigerator, on the coffee table, inside newspapers, etc. You can search for letters randomly or go through the alphabet, searching for the letter *A*, then *B*, then *C*, etc.

Sincerely,

_____

Impresos del ambiente y la lectoescritura

Environmental Print and Literacy

Querida familia,

Los estudios demuestran que cuando los niños interactúan con impresos en su ambiente, esto beneficia su desarrollo de la lectoescritura. Ustedes pueden hacerle notar a su hijo los impresos en su casa y en el vecindario. También pueden mencionar las letras al principio de las palabras y decir los sonidos que esas letras representan. Al fijar la atención de su hijo en las letras y los sonidos de su ambiente, ¡están ayudando a su hijo a reconocer que los impresos están en todas partes! Intenten algunas de las siguientes actividades para divertirse más con los impresos del ambiente.

Cuentos de logotipos

Animen a su hijo a coleccionar los logotipos de sus juguetes, comidas y tiendas favoritas e inclusive de otras de sus cosas favoritas. Guárdenlos en un sobre. De vez en cuando, siéntanse junto a su hijo y hagan que seleccione uno de los logotipos. Peguen el logotipo en una hoja de papel y pídanle a su hijo que invente un cuento sobre él. Escriban el cuento debajo del logotipo mientras su hijo dicta. Pongan los cuentos juntos y hagan un librito con ellos.

Caza de letras

Jueguen a la caza de letras en su casa y busquen tantas letras como puedan encontrar. Animen a su hijo a observar letras que podrían estar en las paredes, en el refrigerador, dentro del refrigerador, en la mesa, en los periódicos, etc. Pueden buscar letras al azar o vayan en orden alfabético, buscando primero la letra *A*, luego *B*, después *C*, etc.

Sinceramente,

_____

Literacy Backpacks

As mentioned in the section on the Roots of Literacy, rich home-literacy environments lead to benefits for children in terms of literacy development. While some families regularly participate in literacy-based activities at home, other families are eager to receive ideas about the kind of activities they can do to enhance literacy learning.

Literacy backpacks are a great way to provide educational opportunities between children and parents. These backpack activities can focus on a variety of literacy topics, including shared reading, reading comprehension, writing development, and language development.

The upcoming pages include instruction sheets to use for several literacy backpacks. You'll find several that have specific literacy activities and one that is generic. This allows you to create a literacy backpack about a topic of your choice. See pages 57–59 for an overview of each backpack activity provided.

Useful Tips for Using Literacy Backpacks

- To create a literacy backpack, you simply provide a few supplies and instructions for how to complete an activity.

- Place the supplies and instructions in a backpack and send it home with a child. Use pillowcases or large resealable plastic bags if backpacks are unavailable.

- It is a good idea to specify a date when the backpack should be returned to school. Use the tracking sheet on page 79 to keep track of each literacy backpack, who has it, and when it is scheduled for return.

- Establish a routine for sending home and collecting backpacks. For example, have children return the backpacks in the morning and send new backpacks home at the end of the day.

- Laminate each backpack instruction sheet for durability.
  Note: The backpack instruction sheet for each activity is provided on pages 60–77 and on the Teacher Resource CD.

- If journals are unavailable, make copies of the journal template on page 78 (also on the Teacher Resource CD) and staple the pages together to make your own journal.

- Introduce and explain the literacy backpacks to families at Back-to-School Night. This will communicate the educational purpose, ensure timely return, and increase overall family participation.

Literacy Backpack Activities

Reading and Writing Fun Backpack

You will need to provide a book, a journal, writing utensils, and a copy of the Reading and Writing Fun Backpack instructions sheet (pages 60–61). This backpack provides families with a way to help build their children's knowledge of story elements (characters, setting, plot, etc.). Families will have the opportunity to discuss the story and write journal entries about what they read.

Counting On Reading Backpack

You will need to provide a book, a journal, writing utensils, a set of manipulatives for counting (paper clips, linking cubes, etc.) in a sealable plastic bag or another kind of container, and a copy of the Counting on Reading Backpack instructions sheet (pages 62–63). The purpose of this backpack is to reinforce children's counting and literacy skills, so it is best to select a book that lends itself to counting.

Let's Write! Backpack

You will need to provide writing utensils (pencils, pens, markers, or chalk), materials to write on (lined paper, construction paper, or a notepad), and a copy of the Let's Write! Backpack instructions sheet (pages 64–65). The purpose of this backpack is to give families the opportunity to write together. You may want to include an envelope filled with sample writing prompts for families to use as a guide. Writing prompts may include such topics as a favorite family meal or a tradition, a story about a family pet, or a special family vacation.

Read It! Make It! Backpack

You will need to provide a book, a container of clay (or salt dough), a disposable camera, and a copy of the Read It! Make It! Backpack instructions sheet (pages 66–67). The purpose of this backpack is to give children and their families the opportunity to reflect on the characters and objects in a story and form them out of clay. Encourage families to capture their creations on film before sending the materials back to school.

Special Visitor Backpack

You will need to provide a book that features an animal, a corresponding stuffed animal, a journal, and a copy of the Special Visitor Backpack instructions letter (pages 68–69). For example, you could send home *Frog and Toad Are Friends* by Arnold Lobel and include a stuffed frog. Families will read the story and write about what the stuffed animal did and saw at the child's house. The stuffed animal could also be used to dramatize the story.

Let's Talk! Backpack

You will need to provide a bag full of mystery objects and the Let's Talk! Backpack instructions letter (pages 70–71). The purpose of this backpack is to get family members to communicate with one another. Each family member will take an item out of the bag and make up a story about it. Another way to use the objects is for one family member to pick an object and begin the story. Then another family member picks a new object and adds to, or continues, the story. This process goes on until there are no more objects to discuss. This is a fun way to introduce creative storytelling and writing.

Let's Make It! Backpack

You will need to provide measuring cups and spoons and simple recipes for families to make and eat together, such as a simple fruit salad, a fun take on a sandwich, or a gelatin dessert. You will also need to include the Let's Make It! Backpack instructions letter (pages 72–73).

Measuring Up! Backpack

You will need to provide a book about size or measurement, a variety of materials that can be used for measurement (ruler, measuring tape, and measuring cups and spoons), a journal, and the Measuring Up! Backpack instructions letter (pages 74–75). Encourage families to measure different things in their homes and draw or write about them in a journal.

Making Music Backpack

You will need to provide a book about music, simple musical instruments (a small drum, a bell, or a shaker) and the Making Music Backpack instructions sheet (pages 76–77). Have families create music together and write about their experiences in a journal. Encourage families to get creative and make their own instruments using materials from around the house to add to those already in the backpack.

Literacy Newsletters

As mentioned earlier in this book, families have an incredible impact on the literacy development of their children. The challenge, however, is that many families do not realize the natural things they can do in the home to encourage this development. In continuing our partnerships with families, it is important for us to offer suggestions to them about the many things they can do at home to engage their children in literacy activities. Remember all of those benefits of family involvement mentioned in the section *What Is Family Involvement?* Keep in mind that those benefits do not refer to involving families at school (although that is still a nice thing to encourage). The benefits to children come mostly from family involvement with their children in the home. On pages 80–101 you will find letters that you can copy and send home to families, offering them information about literacy development and ideas for working with their children. These letters are also available on the Teacher Resource CD.

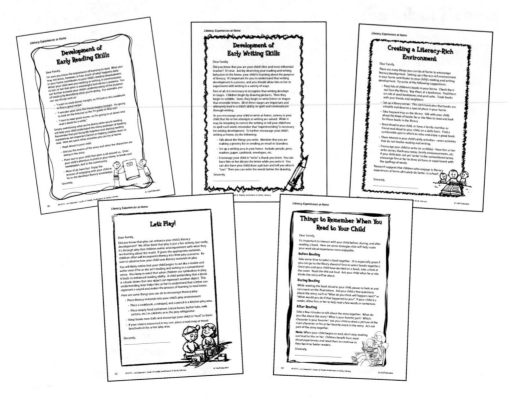

Reading and Writing Fun Backpack

Dear Family,

Congratulations! You and your child have the opportunity to borrow the Reading and Writing Fun Backpack for the next few days. In this backpack, you will find a specially selected book, a journal, and writing utensils. Read the book to your child and then have a discussion about the characters and the events in the story. Then write in the journal about what you both thought about the book. Be sure to include your name and your child's name. Feel free to read the journal entries added by other children and their families. Be sure to return the backpack (with all of the supplies) by the specified date, so it can be sent home with another child. Happy reading!

Sincerely,

_____

Return to school by this date: _____

Materials Included:

- Journal
- Book titled: _____
- Writing utensils: _____
- Other: _____

_____

_____

Mochila de libros y diario

Reading and Writing Fun Backpack

Querida familia:

¡Felicidades! Ustedes y su hijo tienen la oportunidad de que les presten la Mochila de libros y el diario durante los días siguientes. En esta mochila, encontrarán un libro seleccionado especialmente, un diario y objetos para escribir. Leanle el libro a su hijo y luego tengan una conversación sobre los personajes y los eventos del cuento. Luego escriban en el diario sobre lo que opinaron del libro. Asegúrense de incluir su nombre y el nombre de su hijo. No duden en leer las entradas del diario aportadas por otros niños y sus familias. Asegúrense de devolver la mochila (con todos los materiales) para la fecha especificada para que se pueda enviar a la casa de otro niño. ¡Que se diviertan leyendo!

Sinceramente,

_____

La fecha de entrega: _____

Materiales incluidos:

- Diario
- Título del libro: _____
- Objetos para escribir: _____
- Otro: _____

  _____

  _____

Counting On Reading Backpack

Dear Family,

You and your child have the opportunity to borrow the Counting On Reading Backpack. In this backpack, you will find a specially selected book, a journal, writing utensils, and items to use for counting. Read the book to your child and have a discussion about the characters and the events in the story. Try to find items in the story or in the illustrations that can be counted. Use the items in the backpack to count these objects. For example, if there are four children in the story, you might count out four paper clips. Then write in the journal about what your family thought about the book. Be sure to include your name and your child's name. Feel free to read the journal entries added by other children and their families. Be sure to return the backpack (with all of the supplies) by the specified date, so it can be sent home with another child. Happy reading and counting!

Sincerely,

_____

Return to school by this date: _____

Materials Included:

- Journal

- Book titled: _____

- Writing utensils: _____

- Other: _____

_____

_____

Mochila de contar y leer

Counting On Reading Backpack

Querida familia:

Usted y su hijo tienen la oportunidad de que les presten la Mochila de matemáticas y literatura durante los siguientes días. En esta mochila, encontrarán un libro seleccionado especialmente, un diario, utensilios para escribir y objetos que pueden usar para contar. Leale el libro a su hijo y luego tenga una conversación sobre los personajes y los eventos del cuento. Trate de encontrar cosas del cuento o en las ilustraciones que se puedan contar. Use los objetos en la mochila para contar estas cosas. (Por ejemplo, si hay cuatro niños en el cuento, quizás contarían cuatro sujetapapeles.) Luego escriba en el diario acerca de lo que opinaron del libro. Asegúrese de incluir su nombre y el nombre de su hijo. No dude en leer las entradas del diario aportadas por otros niños y sus familias. Asegúrese de devolver la mochila (con todos los materiales) para la fecha especificada para que se pueda enviar a la casa de otro niño. ¡Que se diviertan leyendo y contando!

Sinceramente,

_____

La fecha de entrega: _____

Materiales incluidos:

- Diario
- Título del libro: _____
- Objetos para escribir: _____
- Otro: _____
  _____
  _____

Let's Write! Backpack

Dear Family,

You and your child have the opportunity to borrow the Let's Write! Backpack for the next few days. In this backpack, you will find a variety of writing utensils and different kinds of paper. Spend time writing with your child. Encourage your child to write the words or letters he or she knows. If your child is ready to write sentences, encourage the use of invented spelling. In other words, let your child write the letters he or she hears in the words without worrying about correct spelling. This is a natural part of learning to write. Be sure to return the backpack and supplies by the specified date. Have a great time writing!

Sincerely,

_____

Return to school by this date: _____

Materials Included:

- Journal
- Book titled: _____
- Writing utensils: _____
- Other: _____

_____

_____

Mochila de ¡escribamos!

Let's Write! Backpack

Querida familia:

Usted y su hijo tienen la oportunidad que les presten la Mochila de escritura durante los siguientes días. En esta mochila, encontrarán una variedad de utensilios para escribir y diferentes tipos de papel. Pase tiempo escribiendo con su hijo. Anime a su hijo a escribir las palabras o las letras que sabe. Si su hijo está listo para escribir oraciones, anime el uso de ortografía inventada. En otras palabras, permita que su hijo escriba las letras que oiga en las palabras sin preocuparse de cómo deletree. Esta es una parte natural de las etapas de desarrollo de escritura. Asegúrese de devolver la mochila y los materiales para la fecha especificada. ¡Que se diviertan escribiendo!

Sinceramente,

_____

La fecha de entrega: _____

Materiales incluidos:

- Diario
- Título del libro: _____
- Objetos para escribir: _____
- Otro: _____
  _____
  _____

Read It! Make It! Backpack

Dear Family,

Are you ready for fun? You and your child have the opportunity to borrow the Read It! Make It! Backpack for the next few days. In this backpack, you will find a storybook to read to your child. You will also find some clay and a camera. After reading the book, talk about the story with your child and then use the clay to form characters and objects from the story. Be sure to take one or two pictures of your clay creations with the enclosed camera. When you return the backpack and all of the materials on the specified date, I will have the film developed so we can all see your creations. Get creative!

Sincerely,

_____

Return to school by this date: _____

Materials Included:

- Journal
- Book titled: _____
- Writing utensils: _____
- Other: _____

_____

_____

Mochila de cuentos y arcilla

Read It! Make It! Backpack

Querida familia:

¿Está listo para divertirse? Usted y su hijo tienen la oportunidad de que les presten la Mochila de cuentos y arcilla durante los siguientes días. En esta mochila, encontrarán un libro de cuentos para leerle a su hijo. También encontrarán arcilla y una cámara. Después de leer el libro, hable sobre el cuento y use la arcilla para moldear personajes y objetos del cuento. Asegúrese de sacar una o dos fotografías de sus creaciones de arcilla con la cámara provista. Cuando devuelva la mochila y todos los materiales para la fecha especificada, revelaré el rollo para que todos podamos ver sus creaciones. ¡Sean creativos!

Sinceramente,

_____

La fecha de entrega: _____

Materiales incluidos:

- Diario

- Título del libro: _____

- Objetos para escribir: _____

- Otro: _____

_____

_____

Special Visitor Backpack

Dear Family,

Meet your child's new furry friend! You and your child have the opportunity to borrow the Special Visitor Backpack. In this backpack, you will find a specially selected book and a stuffed animal friend from the story. There is also a writing journal. After reading the story with your child, talk about which character from the book the stuffed animal represents. Write a journal entry together about what the stuffed animal did and saw during its trip to your home. After everyone in the class has made a journal entry, we will be able to read about all of the wonderful places our stuffed animal friend has been! Please be sure to return the backpack on the specified date so it can be sent home with another child.

Have fun!

_____

Return to school by this date: _____

Materials Included:

- Journal
- Book titled: _____
- Writing utensils: _____
- Other: _____

_____

_____

Mochila de un visitante especial

Special Visitor Backpack

Querida familia:

¡Conozca el amigo de peluche nuevo de su niño(a)! Usted y su niño(a) tiene la oportunidad de que le presten el Libro y Mochila de Animal de Peluche. En esta mochila se encuentra un libro especialmente seleccionado y un amigo de peluche del cuento. También hay una carpeta de escritura. Después de leer el cuento con su hijo(a), hable sobre qué personaje del libro representa el animal de peluche. En la carpeta escriba sobre lo que el animal de peluche hizo y vio durante el viaje a su casa. ¡Después de que todos en la clase hayan escrito en la carpeta, podremos leer sobre todos los lugares maravillosos que nuestro amigo de peluche ha visitado! Por favor, asegúrese de devolver la mochila en la fecha indicada para que pueda ser enviada a casa con otro niño(a).

¡Que se diviertan!

_____

La fecha de entrega: _____

Materiales incluidos:

- Diario
- Título del libro: _____
- Objetos para escribir: _____
- Otro: _____

_____

_____

Let's Talk! Backpack

Dear Family,

You and your child have the opportunity to borrow the Let's Talk! Backpack for the next few days. In this backpack, you will find a collection of objects. Use each object to inspire a story! Take one or two items at a time out of the backpack. Take turns with your child telling stories based on the item(s). The stories can be real or make believe. You can also pass an item between you, your child, and other family members. Whoever has the item can make up part of the story and the next person has to pick up where he or she left off. Be creative and have fun! Also, please return the backpack and the enclosed items on the specified date.

Happy story telling!

_____

Return to school by this date: _____

Materials Included:

- Journal
- Book titled: _____
- Writing utensils: _____
- Other: _____

_____

_____

¡Hablemos mochila!

Let's Talk! Backpack

Estimada familia:

En los siguientes días usted y su niño(a) tienen la oportunidad de que le presten Hablemos Mochila. En esta mochila, se encuentra una colección de objetos. ¡Use cada objeto para inspirar un cuento! Saque uno o dos objetos a la vez de la mochila. Tome turnos con su niño(a) contando cuentos basados en este artículo(s). Los cuentos pueden ser reales o de ficción. También puede pasar un objeto entre usted, su hijo(a), y otros miembros de la familia. El que tenga el objeto puede inventar un cuento y la siguiente persona que reciba el objeto tiene que continuar con el cuento donde haya quedado la persona anterior. ¡Se creativo y diviértase! Por favor, asegúrese de devolver la mochila en la fecha indicada.

¡Felices cuentos!

_____

La fecha de entrega: _____

Materiales incluidos:

- Diario
- Título del libro: _____
- Objetos para escribir: _____
- Otro: _____

_____

_____

Let's Make It!
Backpack

Dear Family,

You and your child have the opportunity to borrow the Let's Make It! Backpack for the next few days. In this backpack you will find simple recipes that you can make with your child. Choose a recipe and show your child the list of ingredients. Work together to gather what you need and encourage your child to help with the recipe as much as possible, doing tasks such as pouring and stirring. Then enjoy your creation and encourage your child to feel proud to eat something he or she helped to make! Please return the backpack on the specified date so it can be sent home with another child.

Bon appétit!

_____

Return to school by this date: _____

Materials Included:

- Journal

- Book titled: _____

- Writing utensils: _____

- Other: _____

  _____

  _____

 #50753—An Educator's Guide to Family Involvement in Early Literacy

¡Lo vamos a hacer! Mochila

Let's Make it! Backpack

Estimada familia:

En los siguientes días usted y su niño(a) tienen la oportunidad de que le presten Cocina Mochila. En esta mochila encontrará recetas fáciles que usted puede hacer con su hijo(a). Elija una receta y muéstrele a su hijo(a) la lista de ingredientes. Trabajen juntos para obtener lo que necesiten y anime a su hijo para que le ayude con las tareas de la receta que le sea posible hacer, tal y como vaciar y menear. Continúen y disfruten de su creación y anime a su hijo(a) a sentirse orgulloso de comer algo que él le ayudó a preparar. Por favor, asegúrese de devolver la mochila en la fecha indicada para que pueda ser enviada a casa con otro niño(a).

¡Buen provecho!

_____

La fecha de entrega: _____

Materiales incluidos:

- Diario
- Título del libro: _____
- Objetos para escribir: _____
- Otro: _____

  _____

  _____

Measuring Up!
Backpack

Dear Family,

You and your child have the opportunity to borrow the Measuring Up! Backpack for the next few days. In this backpack you will find various measurement tools and a writing journal. Investigate different items in your home and help your child measure them. How many cups of water will fill the sink? How tall is the front door? How long is the dog's tail? Spark your child's interest by measuring items that he or she enjoys, such as a stuffed animal or book. Record your measurements in the journal and compare them to the journal entries from other families. Please return the backpack on the specified date so other children can investigate with measurement too!

Have fun!

_____

Return to school by this date: _____

Materials Included:

- Journal
- Book titled: _____
- Writing utensils: _____
- Other: _____

_____

_____

Mochila de medidora

Measuring Up! Backpack

Estimada familia:

En los siguientes días usted y su niño(a) tiene la oportunidad de que le presten la Mochila Medidora. En esta mochila se encuentran diversas herramientas de medición y una carpeta de escritura. Investiguen diferentes objetos en su hogar y ayude a su hijo(a) a medirlos. ¿Con cuántas tazas de agua se llenará el fregadero? ¿Qué altura tiene la puerta principal? ¿Qué tan largar es la cola del perro? Anime a su hijo(a) a medir objetos que él o ella disfrutan, tal y como un animal de peluche o un libro. Apunte las medidas en la carpeta y compárelos con lo que otras familias hayan apuntado. Por favor, asegúrese de devolver la mochila en la fecha indicada para que otro niño(a) tenga la oportunidad de investigar midiendo.

¡Que se diviertan!

_____

La fecha de entrega: _____

Materiales incluidos:

- Diario
- Título del libro: _____
- Objetos para escribir: _____
- Otro: _____

_____

_____

Making Music Backpack

Dear Family,

You and your child have the opportunity to borrow the Making Music Backpack for the next few days. In this backpack you will find some simple musical instruments as well as a writing journal. Gather as many family members as you can and give each person an instrument. Have fun making music with your new "band"! Also, let your child experiment with the different instruments to hear the sound that each one makes. Write about your musical experiences in the journal, making sure to include your name and your child's name. Please return the backpack on the specified date.

Have fun!

_____

Return to school by this date: _____

Materials Included:

- Journal
- Book titled: _____
- Writing utensils: _____
- Other: _____

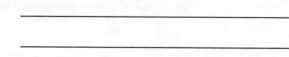

_____

Mochila musical

Making Music Backpack

Estimada familia:

En los próximos días usted y su niño(a) tiene la oportunidad de que le presten la Mochila Musical. En esta mochila se encuentran algunos instrumentos musicales simples y también una carpeta de escritura. Reúna todos los miembros de la familia que pueda y dele a cada uno un instrumento. ¡Diviértase haciendo música con su nueva "banda"! También, deje que su niño(a) experimente con los diferentes instrumentos para escuchar el sonido que cada uno hace. Escriba sobre su experiencia musical en la carpeta y asegúrese de incluir su nombre y el nombre de su hijo(a). Por favor, asegúrese de devolver la mochila en la fecha indicada.

¡Que se diviertan!

_____

La fecha de entrega: _____

Materiales incluidos:

- Diario
- Título del libro:
- Objetos para escribir: _____
  _____
- Otro: _____
  _____
  _____

Journal Page

 #50753—An Educator's Guide to Family Involvement in Early Literacy

Backpack Tracking Sheet

Backpack Topic	Assigned To	Date of Return

Development of Early Reading Skills

Dear Family,

I'm sure you know the importance of learning to read. What you may not know, however, is how much of what happens daily in your home contributes to your child's reading development. When your child sees you reading or writing, it communicates to him or her that print is meaningful and serves a purpose. You can further increase your child's understanding of the purpose of reading by describing what you're doing. For example, you can say things such as:

- "I want to cook dinner tonight, so I'll look in this cookbook to find a good recipe."

- "I wonder what time the movie begins tonight. I'm going to look on the Internet or the TV guide to find out."

- "I love to read good stories, so I'm going to sit down and read a book for a while."

Simply mentioning what you're doing when you're reading will help your child understand the many purposes of reading. Remember that just living life together and sharing reading experiences are important factors in helping children learn to read. Here are some other activities you can try at home:

- Read aloud to your child.

- Discuss the events of the story and what the characters are doing in the story.

- Point out to your child that print is all around us. Draw your child's attention to print in your home, in books and newspapers, and in the community.

- Most of all, have fun! Enjoy the process of engaging with your child as he or she develops literacy knowledge.

Sincerely,

_____

El desarrollo de las primeras habilidades de lectura

Development of Early Reading Skills

Querida familia:

Seguramente sabe la importancia del aprendizaje de la lectura. Lo que quizás no sepa, sin embargo, es qué tanto lo que ocurre en su hogar diariamente contribuye al desarrollo de su hijo en la lectura. Cuando su hijo le observa leyendo o escribiendo, le comunica que el texto es significativo y sirve un propósito. Usted puede aumentar aún más el entendimiento de su hijo del propósito de leer al mencionar lo que usted está haciendo. Por ejemplo, puede decir cosas tales como:

- —Quiero cocinar la cena esta noche, así que buscaré en este libro de cocina para encontrar una buena receta—.
- —Me pregunto a qué hora empieza la película. Voy a buscar en el Internet para averiguarlo—.
- —Me encanta leer buenos cuentos, así que me voy a sentar y leer un libro por un rato—.

Simplemente al mencionar lo que está haciendo cuando está leyendo ayudará a que su hijo entienda los varios propósitos para leer. Recuerde que sólo con vivir juntos y compartir experiencias con la lectura conduce a una transición más exitosa al proceso del aprendizaje en la lectura. Aquí hay otras actividades que puede intentar en casa.

- Leerle en voz alta a su hijo.
- Hablar sobre los eventos del cuento y lo que los personajes hacen en el cuento.
- Hacer que su hijo se de cuenta que los impresos nos rodean. Hacerle notar a su hijo los impresos en su hogar, en los libros y los periódicos y en la comunidad.
- Sobre todo, ¡diviértanse! Disfrute del proceso de interactuar con su hijo conforme desarrolla conocimiento en la lectoescritura.

Sinceramente,

_____

Development of Early Writing Skills

Dear Family,

Did you know that *you* are your child's first and most influential teacher? It's true. Just by observing your reading and writing behaviors in the home, your child is learning about the purpose of literacy. It's important for you to understand that writing development is a *process*, and you should allow him or her to experiment with writing in a variety of ways.

First of all, it is necessary to recognize that writing develops in stages. Children begin by drawing pictures. Then they begin to scribble. Soon, they begin to write letters or shapes that resemble letters. All of these stages are important and ultimately lead to a child's ability to spell and communicate through writing.

As you encourage your child to write at home, convey to your child that his or her attempts at writing are valued. While it may be tempting to correct the writing or tell your child how to spell each word, remember that "experimenting" is necessary for writing development. To further encourage your child's writing at home, try the following:

- Talk about the things you write. Mention that you are making a grocery list or sending an email to Grandma.

- Set up a writing area in your home. Include pencils, pens, markers, paper, cardstock, envelopes, etc.

- Encourage your child to "write" a thank-you letter. You can have him or her dictate the letter while you write it. You can also have your child draw a picture and tell you what it "says." Then you can write the words below the drawing.

Sincerely,

_____

El desarrollo de las primeras habilidades de escritura

Development of Early Writing Skills

Querida familia:

¿Sabía que USTED es el primer y el más influyente maestro que tiene su hijo? Es verdad. Sólo con observar los comportamientos de la lectoescritura en el hogar, su hijo aprende sobre el propósito de la lectoescritura. Es importante que usted entienda que el desarrollo de la escritura es un proceso y debería permitir que su hijo experimente con la escritura en una variedad de maneras.

Lo primero es que es necesario reconocer que la escritura se desarrolla en etapas. Los niños empiezan haciendo dibujos. Luego empiezan a garabatear. Pronto empiezan a escribir letras o figuras que parecen letras. Todas estas etapas son importantes y al final conducen a la habilidad de un niño a deletrear y comunicarse a través de la escritura.

Conforme anime a su hijo a escribir en casa, hágale saber que sus intentos para escribir se valoran. Aunque sea tentador corregir la escritura o decirle a su hijo cómo deletrear cada palabra, recuerde que este proceso de experimentación es necesario para el desarrollo de la escritura. Para animar más a su hijo a escribir en casa, trate de hacer lo siguiente:

- Hable sobre las cosas que escriba. Mencione que está haciendo una lista de compras o enviándole un correo electrónico a la Abuela.

- Establezca un área de escritura en su hogar. Incluya lápices, plumas, marcadores, papel, tarjetas, sobres, etc.

- Anime a su hijo a "escribir" una carta de agradecimiento. Puede hacer que su hijo le dicte la carta mientras usted la escribe. También puede hacer que su hijo haga un dibujo, que le comunique lo que "diga", y usted puede escribir las palabras debajo del dibujo.

Sinceramente,

_____

Creating a Literacy-Rich Environment

Dear Family,

There are many things you can do at home to encourage literacy development. Setting up a literacy-rich environment in your home contributes to your child's reading and writing development. Try some of the following suggestions:

- Keep lots of children's books in your home. Check them out from the library. Buy them at a bookstore. Find them on sale at used bookstores and yard sales. Trade books with your friends and neighbors.

- Set up a library corner. This communicates that books are valuable and deserve a special place in your home.

- Take frequent trips to the library. Talk with your child about the kinds of books he or she likes to read and look for those books in the library.

- Read aloud to your child, or have a family member or friend read aloud to your child, on a daily basis. Find a comfortable spot in which to relax and enjoy a good book.

- Show interest in your child's daily activities—even activities that do not involve reading and writing.

- Encourage your child to write (or scribble). Have him or her write stories, thank-you notes, family announcements, etc. If your child does not yet "write" in the conventional sense, encourage him or her to draw pictures or experiment with the spellings of words.

Research suggests that children who engage in literacy experiences at home ultimately do better in school!

Sincerely,

_____

La creación de un ambiente rico en la lectoescritura

Creating a Literacy-Rich Environment

Querida familia:

Hay muchas cosas que puede hacer en el hogar para animar el desarrollo de la lectoescritura. Establecer un ambiente rico en la lectoescritura en su hogar contribuye al desarrollo de la lectura y la escritura. Intente algunas de estas estrategias en su hogar:

- Mantenga muchos libros para niños en su hogar. Puede pedirlos prestados de la biblioteca. Puede comprarlos en una librería. Puede encontrarlos rebajados en librerías con libros de segunda mano y ventas de cochera. Intercambie libros con sus amigos y vecinos.

- Establezca una biblioteca en un rincón en su hogar. Esto comunica que los libros son valiosos y que merecen un lugar especial en la biblioteca.

- Leale a su hijo diariamente. Encuentre un lugar cómodo en el que puedan acurrucarse y disfrutar de un buen libro.

- Exprese interés en las actividades diarias de su hijo—inclusive las actividades que no se traten de la lectura y la escritura.

- Anime a su hijo a escribir (o garabatear). Haga que escriba cuentos, cartas de agradecimiento, anuncios familiares, etc. Si su hijo todavía no sabe "escribir" en el sentido convencional, anímele a hacer dibujos o experimentar con la ortografía de las palabras. ¡La investigación sugiere que los niños que se involucran en experiencias de la lectoescritura en casa, tienen más éxito en la escuela!

Sinceramente,

_____

Let's Play!

Dear Family,

Did you know that play can enhance your child's literacy development? We often think that play is just a fun activity, but really, it's through play that children mimic and experiment with what they are learning about the world. If given the appropriate materials, children often will incorporate literacy into their play scenarios. Be sure to observe how your child uses literacy materials in play.

You will likely notice that your child begins to act like a reader and writer even if he or she isn't reading and writing in a conventional sense. Also keep in mind that when children use symbolism in play, it leads to enhanced reading ability. A child pretending that a block is a book shows that one object can represent another object. This understanding later helps him or her to understand that a letter can represent a sound and makes the process of learning to read easier.

Here are some things you can do to encourage literacy play:

- Place literacy materials into your child's play environment.
  - Place a cookbook, a notepad, and a pencil in a kitchen play area.
  - Place empty food containers (cereal boxes, butter tubs, milk cartons, etc.) in cabinets or in the play refrigerator.
- Keep books near dolls and encourage your child to "read" to them.
- If your child is interested in toy cars, place a road map or travel brochures in his or her play area.

Sincerely,

_____

¡Juguemos!

Let's Play!

Querida familia:

¿Sabía que los juegos pueden fomentar el desarrollo de la lectoescritura de su hijo? Solemos pensar que los juegos son actividades mecánicas, pero a través de los juegos, los niños imitan y experimentan con lo que están aprendiendo sobre el mundo. La investigación nos dice que si se proporcionan los materiales apropiados, los niños están más propuestos a incorporar la lectoescritura en sus escenarios de juego. Asegúrese de observar cómo su hijo usa materiales de la lectoescritura en sus juegos.

Usted probablemente notará que su hijo empezará a comportarse como un lector y un escritor aunque no esté leyendo ni escribiendo en un sentido convencional. También tenga en cuenta que cuando los niños usan el simbolismo en sus juegos, conduce a las habilidades mejoradas de lectura. Un niño que imagina que un bloque es un libro representa que un objeto simboliza algo diferente. Este entendimiento ayuda más tarde a que su hijo entienda que una letra puede representar un sonido y facilita el proceso del aprendizaje de lectura.

Aquí hay algunas cosas que puede hacer para animar juegos de lectoescritura:

- Llene el ambiente de juegos que usa su hijo con materiales de lectoescritura. Coloque un libro de cocina, un bloc de notas y un lápiz en un área de juego en la cocina. Coloque recipientes vacíos de alimentos (cajas de cereal, cajas de mantequilla, etc.) en los armarios de la cocina o en el refrigerador imaginario.

- Mantenga libros cerca de los muñecos y anime a su hijo a que les "lea" esos libros.

- Si su hijo se interesa por los carros de juguete, coloque un mapa o folletos de viaje en su área de juego.

Sinceramente,

_____

Beginning, Middle, End

Dear Family,

As a great follow-up for reading aloud to your child, have a discussion about the events that happened at the beginning, middle, and end of the story. The questions below can guide your discussion. Along with your child, create a sentence that tells about the beginning of the story and write it down on the lines provided. When you have finished answering the questions, ask your child to draw a picture to go with it.

What happened at the beginning of the story?

_____

_____

What happened in the middle of the story?

_____

_____

What happened at the end of the story?

_____

_____

Draw a picture of your favorite part.

Sincerely,

_____

#50753—An Educator's Guide to Family Involvement in Early Literacy   © Shell Education

Principio, desarrollo, final

Beginning, Middle, End

Querida familia:

Como buena continuación con la lectura después de la lectura inicial en voz alta, tenga una conversación sobre los eventos que suceden al principio, en el desarrollo y al final del cuento. Las preguntas que siguen pueden guiar su conversación. Junto con su hijo, crea una oración que relate el principio del cuento. Escríbala en el cuadro y luego pídale a su hijo que haga un dibujo que la acompañe.

¿Qué sucede al principio del cuento?

_____

_____

¿Qué sucede durante el desarrollo del cuento?

_____

_____

¿Qué sucede al final del cuento?

_____

_____

Haz un dibujo de tu parte favorita.

Sinceramente,

_____

Great Authors

Dear Family,

You know that reading to your child is a great thing, but do you ever wonder *what* to read? You can start by looking for books by popular children's book authors. Take a look at the list below. You'll find authors and a few of their books. But don't stop there! There are many more wonderful children's books that you and your child can enjoy together.

Allan Ahlberg
- *The Jolly Postman or Other People's Letters*

Eric Carle
- *The Grouchy Ladybug*
- *The Very Hungry Caterpillar*

Arnold Lobel
- *Frog and Toad Are Friends*
- *Frog and Toad Together*

Patricia McKissack
- *Mirandy and Brother Wind*

Gary Soto
- *Too Many Tamales*
- *If the Shoe Fits*

Audrey Wood
- *The Napping House*
- *Silly Sally*

Sincerely,

_____

Buenos autores

Great Authors

Querida familia:

Ya sabe que leerle a su hijo es una cosa magnífica, ¿pero se pregunta *qué* debe leerle? Puede empezar al buscar libros escritos por autores populares en el género de libros para niños. Vea la lista siguiente. Encontrará autores y unos de sus libros. Pero ¡no se detenga allí! Hay muchos libros para niños fascinantes que usted y su hijo pueden disfrutar juntos.

Allan Ahlberg
- *The Jolly Postman or Other People's Letters*

Eric Carle
- *The Grouchy Ladybug*
- *The Very Hungry Caterpillar*

Arnold Lobel
- *Frog and Toad Are Friends*
- *Frog and Toad Together*

Patricia McKissack
- *Mirandy and Brother Wind*

Gary Soto
- *Too Many Tamales*
- *If the Shoe Fits*

Audrey Wood
- *The Napping House*
- *Silly Sally*

Sinceramente,

_____

More Great Authors

Dear Family,

I hope you've been able to find some fun books to read to your child. Here is another list of great authors and their books. Happy reading!

Janell Cannon
- *Pinduli*
- *Stellaluna*

Bill Martin Jr.
- *Brown Bear, Brown Bear, What Do You See?*
- *Chicka Chicka Boom Boom*

Mercer Meyer
- *There's a Nightmare in My Closet*
- *What Do You Do with a Kangaroo?*

Laura Numeroff
- *If You Give a Mouse a Cookie*
- *If You Give a Moose a Muffin*

Mo Willems
- *Don't Let the Pigeon Drive the Bus!*
- *The Pigeon Finds a Hot Dog!*

Jane Yolen
- *Greyling*
- *Owl Moon*

Sincerely,

_____

Más buenos autores

More Great Authors

Querida familia:

Espero que haya podido encontrar algunos libros divertidos que pueda leerle a su hijo. Aquí hay otra lista de grandes autores y sus libros. ¡Que se diviertan leyendo!

Janell Cannon
- *Pinduli*
- *Stellaluna*

Bill Martin Jr.
- *Brown Bear, Brown Bear, What Do You See?*
- *Chicka Chicka Boom Boom*

Mercer Meyer
- *There's a Nightmare in My Closet*
- *What Do You Do with a Kangaroo?*

Laura Numeroff
- *If You Give a Mouse a Cookie*
- *If You Give a Moose a Muffin*

Mo Willems
- *Don't Let the Pigeon Drive the Bus!*
- *The Pigeon Finds a Hot Dog!*

Jane Yolen
- *Greyling*
- *Owl Moon*

Sinceramente,

_____

Great Children's Poets

Dear Family,

Reading poetry to children is great fun! By listening to poetry, children can learn a variety of skills that will lead to reading success. As you read, invite your child to chime in with rhyming or repetitive words. Be sure to read his or her favorite poems over and over again. Take a look at the list below for great children's poets and a few of their works. Then, off to the library!

Jack Prelutsky
- *A Pizza the Size of the Sun*
- *The Random House Book of Poetry for Children*
- *Read-Aloud Rhymes for the Very Young*
- *Read a Rhyme, Write a Rhyme*
- *Something Big Has Been Here*

Shel Silverstein
- *A Light in the Attic*
- *Falling Up*
- *Where the Sidewalk Ends*

Robert Louis Stevenson
- *A Child's Garden of Verses*

Judith Viorst
- *If I Were in Charge of the World (and Other Worries)*

Nadine Bernard Westcott
- *Never Take a Pig to Lunch (and Other Poems about the Fun of Eating)*

Sincerely,

_____

Buenos poetas de poesía para los niños

Great Children's Poets

Querida familia:

¡Leerle poesía a los niños es bastante divertido! Al escuchar poesía, los niños pueden aprender una variedad de destrezas que conducirán al éxito en la lectura. Mientras lee, invite a su hijo a unirse con la lectura diciendo palabras que riman o palabras repetitivas. Asegúrese de leer sus poemas favoritos una y otra vez. Vea en la lista siguiente buenos poetas en el género de poesía para niños y unas de sus obras. Luego, ¡visite la biblioteca!

Jack Prelutsky
- *A Pizza the Size of the Sun*
- *The Random House Book of Poetry for Children*
- *Read-Aloud Rhymes for the Very Young*
- *Read a Rhyme, Write a Rhyme*
- *Something Big Has Been Here*

Shel Silverstein
- *A Light in the Attic*
- *Falling Up*
- *Where the Sidewalk Ends*

Robert Louis Stevenson
- *A Child's Garden of Verses*

Judith Viorst
- *If I Were in Charge of the World (and Other Worries)*

Nadine Bernard Westcott
- *Never Take a Pig to Lunch (and Other Poems about the Fun of Eating)*

Sinceramente,

_____

Reading and Singing

Dear Family,

Reading and singing go well together. When children participate in singing, they learn a lot about language and reading. A great way to engage in singing activities together is to read (and sing) books. Take a look at the list below to find authors and books that include easy to sing (and easy to read) books.

Alan Katz and David Catrow

- *Are You Quite Polite?*
- *Take Me Out of the Bathtub*

Mary Ann Hoberman

- *I Know an Old Lady Who Swallowed a Fly*
- *Skip to My Lou*

John Langstaff

- *Oh, A-Hunting We Will Go*
- *Over in the Meadow*

Raffi

- *Baby Beluga*
- *Down by the Bay*
- *Shake My Sillies Out*

Nadine Bernard Westcott

- *The Lady with the Alligator Purse*
- *Peanut Butter and Jelly: A Play Rhyme*

Sincerely,

_____

Leer y cantar

Reading and Singing

Querida familia:

Leer y cantar se complementan. Cuando los niños participan en el acto de cantar, aprenden mucho sobre el lenguaje y la lectura. Una buena manera para experimentar con actividades de cantar juntos es leer (y cantar) los libros. Vea la lista siguiente para encontrar autores y libros que incluyen libros que son fáciles de cantar (y fáciles de leer).

Alan Katz and David Catrow

- *Are You Quite Polite?*
- *Take Me Out of the Bathtub*

Mary Ann Hoberman

- *I Know an Old Lady Who Swallowed a Fly*
- *Skip to My Lou*

John Langstaff

- *Oh, A-Hunting We Will Go*
- *Over in the Meadow*

Raffi

- *Baby Beluga*
- *Down by the Bay*
- *Shake My Sillies Out*

Nadine Bernard Westcott

- *The Lady with the Alligator Purse*
- *Peanut Butter and Jelly: A Play Rhyme*

Sinceramente,

_____

Things to Remember When You Read to Your Child

Dear Family,

It's important to interact with your child before, during, and after reading a book. Here are some strategies that will help make your read-aloud experience more enjoyable.

Before Reading

Take some time to select a book together. (It is especially great if you can go to the library ahead of time to select books together.) Once you and your child have decided on a book, take a look at the cover. Read the title out loud. Ask your child what he or she thinks the story will be about.

During Reading

While reading the book aloud to your child, pause to look at and comment on the illustrations. Ask your child a few questions about the story, such as "What do you think will happen next?" or "What would you do if that happened to you?" If your child is a reader, allow him or her to help read a few words or sentences.

After Reading

Take a few minutes to talk about the story together. What do you like about the story? What is your favorite part? Which character is your favorite? Ask your child to draw a picture of the main character or his or her favorite event in the story. Act out part of the story together.

Note: When your child begins to read, don't stop reading out loud to him or her. Children benefit from read-aloud experiences and need them to continue as they become better readers.

Sincerely,

_____

Cosas que recordar cuando le lea a su hijo

Things to Remember When You Read to Your Child

Querida familia,

Es importante interactuar con su hijo antes, durante y después de leer un libro. Aquí hay unas estrategias que ayudarán a crear una experiencia más agradable de la lectura en voz alta.

Antes de la lectura

Pase suficiente tiempo seleccionando un libro juntos. (Es especialmente bueno si pueden ir a la biblioteca de adelantado para seleccionar libros juntos.) En cuanto usted y su hijo hayan decidido qué libro escoger, miren la portada. Lea el título en voz alta. Preguntele a su hijo de qué piensa que se tratará el libro.

Durante la lectura

Mientras le lee el libro en voz alta a su hijo, pause para observar y hacer comentarios sobre las ilustraciones. Hagale a su hijo unas preguntas sobre el cuento, tal como —¿Qué piensas que sucederá ahora?— o —¿Qué harías si eso te sucediera a ti?— Si su hijo puede leer, permita que lea algunas palabras u oraciones.

Después de la lectura

Tome unos minutos para hablar juntos sobre el cuento. ¿Cuáles partes les gusta? ¿Cuál es su parte favorita? ¿Qué personaje es tu favorito? Pídale a su hijo que haga un dibujo del personaje principal o de su evento favorito del cuento. Representen juntos una parte del cuento.

Nota: Cuando su hijo empiece a leer, no pare de leerle en voz alta. Los niños se benefician de experiencias en las cuales escuchan una lectura de un libro y las necesitan seguido conforme llegan a ser mejores lectores.

Sinceramente,

_____

Let's Talk!

Dear Family,

Having conversations with your child is a great way to show your child that you value his or her thoughts. It's also a great way to promote language development and just enjoy each other's company. Here are some activities you can do at home to promote your child's language development.

Car Talk

While you are driving around doing errands, ask your child about his or her day. What did he or she do? What made him or her happy? Point out objects or people in the environment and ask your child what he or she thinks about them.

Dinner Talk

Encourage conversation at the dinner table. Ask each family member to share something that happened that day. If you ask, "What did you do today?" you may hear your child say, "Nothing." Don't get discouraged. If you ask specific questions, your child is likely to respond. Here are some questions to get you started:

- What book did you read today?
- What happened on the playground?
- What did you learn about in science?
- Tell me about your friend, _____ (Katie, for example).

Story Talk

Engage in storytelling with your child. You can start by making up a story about any character or topic. Invite your child to add parts to the story. Then ask your child to make up a story to tell.

Sincerely,

_____

¡Hablemos!

Let's Talk!

Querida familia:

Tener conversaciones con su hijo es una buena manera de mostrarle a su hijo que usted valora sus pensamientos. También es una buena manera de promover el desarrollo del lenguaje y de simplemente disfrutar la compañía uno del otro. Aquí hay unas actividades que puede hacer en casa para promover el desarrollo del lenguaje de su hijo.

Hablar en el carro

Mientras conduce a los lugares para hacer mandados, preguntele a su hijo sobre cómo le fue el día. ¿Qué hizo? ¿Qué le hizo sentirse feliz? Hágale fijarse en objetos o personas en su entorno y preguntele a su hijo qué opina.

Hablar durante la cena

Anime a su familia a tener conversaciones durante la cena. Pídale a cada miembro de la familia que comparta algo que sucedió ese día. Si le pregunta, —¿Qué hiciste hoy?—, es posible que su hijo diga —Nada—. No se decepcione. Si usted le hace preguntas específicas, su hijo probablemente responderá. Aquí hay algunas preguntas para empezar:

- ¿Qué libro leíste hoy?
- ¿Qué pasó en el patio de recreo?
- ¿Sobre qué aprendiste en la clase de ciencias?
- Dime sobre tu amiga, _____ (Katie, por ejemplo).

Hablar sobre los cuentos

Cuente historias con su hijo. Puede empezar al inventar un cuento sobre cualquier personaje o tema. Invite a su hijo a agregar partes al cuento. Luego pídale a su hijo que invente un cuento y que se lo diga.

Sinceramente,

_____

Notes

 #50753—*An Educator's Guide to Family Involvement in Early Literacy*

Family Literacy Workshops

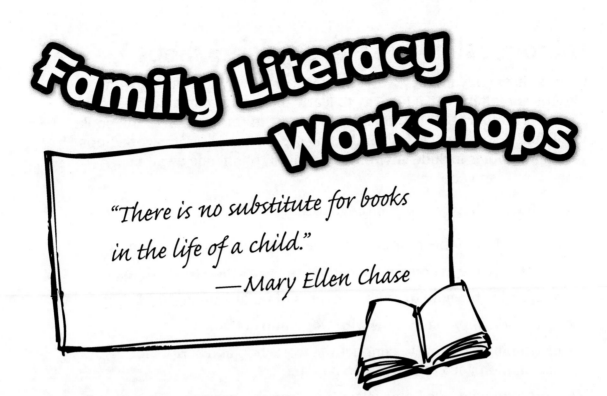

"There is no substitute for books in the life of a child."

—Mary Ellen Chase

Family Literacy

Introduction to Literacy Workshops

Conducting family literacy workshops is a great way to connect with parents and offer them a fun way to learn about engaging activities they can do to support their children's education. In this section of the book, you'll find detailed plans for conducting six different literacy workshops. Workshop topics include environmental print, phonemic awareness, read-alouds, and cooking.

For each workshop, you'll find the following:

- an overview of the information to be presented in the workshop
- a reproducible announcement about the workshop to send home
- a reproducible note to remind parents of the upcoming workshop
- an agenda for you to follow with workshop activities
- instructions for how to conduct the workshop and scripts for information you can provide to parents
- a reproducible take-home letter that provides parents with information and more ideas to take home

Feel free to adapt the workshops so that they meet the needs of your families. Some of the workshops lend themselves to family-child participation, while others are best suited as a means of working solely with families to create materials that they can use at home. You may want to indicate on the initial workshop announcement whether children are invited to attend. While not mandatory, you can increase the likelihood of family attendance by offering food and childcare. If only a few parents attend the first workshop, don't be discouraged. Once other parents hear about the great information and fun activities other parents received, you are likely to see increased attendance at future workshops.

Environmental Print Workshop

You may recall from earlier in this book that environmental print refers to familiar print in a child's surroundings. Street signs, product labels, restaurant and store signs, and logos on toys are all considered environmental print. Environmental print conveys to children that print is meaningful and functional. Research further indicates that, with the assistance of an adult, a child will begin to notice individual letters within environmental-print logos when attention is drawn to them (Prior and Gerard 2004): "Using these highly motivating and visually appealing materials creates a meaningful foundation for learning about the alphabetic principle" (9).

This workshop focuses helping families learn how to use environmental print to help develop their children's literacy skills. The activities are fun, engaging, and easy to do.

The environmental print workshop includes the following:

- an agenda (page 106)
- detailed instructions and a script (pages 106–109)
- an invitation (pages 110–111)
- reminder notes (pages 112–113)
- take-home letter (pages 114–115)

Note: It is a good idea to send the workshop invitation home to families at least one week prior to the event. Then send the reminder note home at least three days prior to the event.

Estimated time: 1 hour, 15 minutes

Number of activities: 3

Materials and preparation required: Yes (see instructions)

Adults only: Yes

If you find that this workshop is a success and parents are interested, you might want to create an additional workshop and invite parents to bring their children. Families can try out their environmental-print games and even use some new ones with their children.

Environmental Print Workshop

Agenda

Welcome/Introductions (5–10 minutes)

What Is Environmental Print? (5 minutes)

Group Interaction (5 minutes)

Activity 1: Cereal Box Puzzles (10 minutes)

Activity 2: Two-Piece Puzzles (20 minutes)

Activity 3: Memory Game (20 minutes)

Questions/Share Ideas (5 minutes)

Welcome

Begin by welcoming parents and allowing time for families to introduce themselves to one another. You may even want to provide snacks for participants.

What Is Environmental Print?

Take a few minutes to tell the group about the focus of the workshop (environmental print) and that they will have the chance to create some activities that they can use at home with their children. Use the script below to assist you:

This workshop is about using environmental print to help your child develop early reading skills. What is environmental print? Does anyone want to guess? (Allow families to respond.) Environmental print is the print all around us. When we talk about it in terms of education, we are referring to the print that children recognize even before they are able to read. You have probably noticed that your child recognizes the names of cereals, stores, toys, and maybe even street signs. When your child recognizes environmental print, it communicates that print is meaningful and serves a purpose. If you draw your child's attention to environmental print in your home and in the community, you are helping him or her to develop a better understanding of the purpose and function of print. We can even use environmental print games to draw children's attention to letters and sounds. In this workshop, I'm going to show you some fun ways that you and your child can play together using environmental print.

Group Interaction

Provide each family member with an index card and a pencil. Ask each person to list examples of print, in the home and community, that they think their children recognize. Encourage parents to work together to come up with ideas for their lists. After they have had a few minutes to make their lists, allow parents to share with the whole group.

Activity 1: Cereal Box Puzzles

Materials:
- empty cereal boxes
- scissors
- sealable plastic bags

Explain to parents that an easy way to draw children's attention to letters is to make puzzles from product packaging. They can use old pizza boxes, laundry detergent boxes, and cereal boxes. All they have to do is cut out the front panel of the box and then cut the box into seven or eight pieces. The child then assembles the puzzle. Tell parents that children will often look at the letters that have been cut apart or in half and mention putting them back together. For example, a child might say, "There's the top of the *C*."

Distribute a cereal box, scissors, and a plastic bag to each family. Allow a few minutes for families to create their puzzles. Encourage them to store the puzzle pieces in the sealable plastic bag.

Activity 2: Two-Piece Puzzles

Materials:
- 9" x 13" construction paper (one sheet for each family member)
- scissors
- glue
- logos (four for each parent) and a matching letter for each logo
- sealable plastic bags

Preparation: Select four recognizable logos (such as Cheerios®, LEGO®, Band-Aid®, and Sesame Street®). Using a color printer, print the logos and the beginning letter of each logo (*C, L, B, S*). Each family member should have one copy of each logo and beginning letter.

Instructions: Explain to parents that they will make four two-piece puzzles. The purpose of the activity is for a child to match a logo to the puzzle piece with the matching beginning letter. Instruct each parent to fold the sheet of construction paper in half and then in half again, making four rectangles. Then have the parent cut the rectangles apart. The parent glues a logo at the top of the rectangle and the matching letter at the bottom. Then the parent cuts the rectangle in half, using a jagged puzzle-type edge. The parent continues in the same manner with the remaining logos and letters. (Use the plastic bags for storage.) Explain to parents that when playing, the puzzle pieces are mixed up and the child assembles the puzzles by matching logos to their beginning letters. Tell parents that they should engage their children in discussion about the letters in the logos and the sounds they hear when the letters are pronounced.

Activity 3: Memory Game

Materials:
- 9" x 13" construction paper (two sheets for each family member)
- scissors
- logos (four for each parent) and the typed word for each logo
- sealable plastic bags
- glue

Preparation: Select four different logos that the children will recognize. Using a color printer, print the logos. Then type each logo word in a large font size and print out copies for each family.

Instructions: To play, all cards are mixed up and then placed facedown on a tabletop or floor. The child turns over two cards, attempting to match a logo to the matching typed word. If the child makes a match, he or she keeps the cards. If a match is not made, the child turns the cards over and tries again.

Note: Try to select logos that are different from the ones selected for the two-piece puzzle activity.

Questions/Share Ideas

After finishing the three activities, allow a few minutes for families to "debrief," sharing their thoughts, ideas, and questions. Ask them where they might locate familiar logos and how they might use these activities at home. Encourage them to maintain a playlike environment when using the materials, rather than feeling the need to take on the role of teacher. The purpose of using the materials is to show interest in the child's literacy development with fun and engaging activities.

Note: For those families who need more time, encourage them to complete the activity at home.

Take-Home Letter

Finally, distribute copies of the Environmental Print Take-Home Letter. Explain that this letter will remind families of a few things which they learned in the workshop and offer a few more suggestions for using environmental print with their children.

Note: If you plan to send home the environmental print take-home letter found on pages 114–115 and on the Teacher Resource CD, mention this to parents so they can expect more ideas in future weeks.

Environmental Print Workshop

Dear Families,

You're invited to a family reading workshop. You will learn how to use print items around the house to help your child develop early reading skills. This workshop is for parents or other adults only. Please no children.

Date: _____

Time: _____

Location: _____

Please let us know if you plan to come:

Contact Name: _____

Phone/Email: _____

Sincerely,

_____

Taller de impresos del ambiente

Environmental Print Workshop

Querida familia:

Le invitamos a un taller de lectura con su familia. Aprenderá a usar impresos alrededor de la casa para ayudar a su hijo a desarrollar las primeras habilidades de lectura. Este taller es para adultos u otros adultos solamente. Por favor no niños.

Fecha: _____

Hora: _____

Lugar: _____

Avísenos si piensa venir:

Nombre de contacto: _____

Número de teléfono/Correo electrónico:

_____

Sinceramente,

_____

Don't Forget!

Don't forget, we're having a family reading night! Come join us to learn about fun ways you can enhance your child's beginning reading skills. Adults only please!

Date: _____

Time: _____

Location: _____

Don't Forget!

Don't forget, we're having a family reading night! Come join us to learn about fun ways you can enhance your child's beginning reading skills. Adults only please!

Date: _____

Time: _____

Location: _____

Don't Forget!

Don't forget, we're having a family reading night! Come join us to learn about fun ways you can enhance your child's beginning reading skills. Adults only please!

Date: _____

Time: _____

Location: _____

Don't Forget!

Don't forget, we're having a family reading night! Come join us to learn about fun ways you can enhance your child's beginning reading skills. Adults only please!

Date: _____

Time: _____

Location:

¡No se olvide!

No se olvide de la noche de lectura con la familia. Venga a participar y aprender sobre divertidas maneras para mejorar las habilidades de lectura de su hijo.

Fecha _____

Hora: _____

Lugar: _____

¡No se olvide!

No se olvide de la noche de lectura con la familia. Venga a participar y aprender sobre divertidas maneras para aumentar las habilidades de lectura de su hijo.

Fecha: _____

Hora: _____

Lugar: _____

¡No se olvide!

No se olvide de la noche de lectura con la familia. Venga a participar y aprender sobre divertidas maneras para mejorar las habilidades de lectura de su hijo.

Fecha: _____

Hora: _____

Lugar: _____

¡No se olvide!

No se olvide de la noche de lectura con la familia. Venga a participar y aprender sobre divertidas maneras para mejorar las habilidades de lectura de su hijo.

Fecha: _____

Hora: _____

Lugar: _____

Environmental Print Workshop Take-Home Letter

Dear Family,

Thank you for attending the Environmental Print Workshop. I hope that you and your child will enjoy using the games you made. Remember that environmental print refers to the print, signs, logos, and labels that your child recognizes in your home and community. By pointing out this familiar print and drawing your child's attention to the letters and sounds in the text, your child will begin to recognize that print is meaningful and that it is made up of individual letters and sounds. These brief interactions with your child will enhance his or her overall development of beginning reading skills. As you focus on environmental print in the coming weeks and months, try some of these activities:

- Point out print while driving down the road.

- When your child selects a favorite cereal, ask him or her to identify the first letter in the logo.

- Ask your child to listen for the beginning sound in a logo. For example, rather than just identifying that LEGO® begins with the letter *L*, have your child make the sound that *L* makes.

- Ask your child to identify the names of stores, products, streets, etc., simply by looking at the signs and labels.

Be sure to have fun interacting with your child as he or she explores literacy. You will likely find that these activities are enjoyable, motivating, and positively affecting their learning of letters and sounds. Most of all, you will see that your child now has an enormous literacy resource open to him or her—the world!

Sincerely,

_____

Juice

Carta para llevar a casa sobre los impresos del ambiente

Environmental Print Workshop Take-Home Letter

Querida familia:

Gracias por asistir al taller de los impresos del ambiente. Espero que disfrute usar los juegos que hizo con su hijo. Recuerde que los impresos del ambiente se refiere al texto, los letreros, los logotipos y las etiquetas que su hijo reconoce en su hogar y la comunidad. Cuando hace que su hijo se fije en estos impresos familiares y las letras y los sonidos en el texto, su hijo empezará a reconocer que los impresos tienen significado y que están hechos de letras y sonidos individuales. Estas interacciones breves con su hijo aumentarán su desarrollo de primeras habilidades de lectura. Mientras usted se enfoca en los impresos del entorno en las semanas y los meses que vienen, intente algunas de estas actividades:

- Haga que su hijo se fije en los impresos mientras conduce por las calles.

- Cuando su hijo escoja un cereal favorito, pídale que identifique la primera letra en el logotipo.

- Pídale a su hijo que intente escuchar el sonido inicial en un logotipo. Por ejemplo, en vez de sólo identificar que LEGO® empieza con la letra *L*, haga que su hijo diga el sonido de la letra *L*.

- Pídale a su hijo que identifique los nombres de tiendas, productos, calles, etc., simplemente con mirar los letreros y etiquetas.

Asegúrese de divertirse interactuando con su hijo mientras explora la lectoescritura. Probablemente encontrará que estas actividades son divertidas, motivadoras y que influencian positivamente su aprendizaje de letras y sonidos. De mayor importancia, usted verá que el enorme recurso de la lectoescritura le ha abierto a su hijo—¡el mundo!

Sinceramente,

_____

Juice

Phonemic Awareness Workshop

Phonemic awareness is the ability to hear, identify, and manipulate the individual sounds in spoken words. Unlike phonics, it does not focus on letters, but rather on the sounds of speech. Children who have developed phonemic awareness have the ability to reflect on features of spoken language. They recognize that spoken words are made up of sounds. They also recognize that words can rhyme and that words can be changed in order to make new words. Phonemic awareness is important as a precursor to learning letters and their sounds. It helps children to realize that there is a purpose for learning to read because they are able to understand that text represents spoken language (Yopp and Yopp 2000).

Because phonemic awareness is so important in the process of learning to read, it makes sense to conduct a workshop for parents explaining what phonemic awareness is and how they can participate in this process with their children.

The phonemic awareness workshop includes the following:

- an agenda (page 117)
- detailed instructions and a script (pages 117–120)
- an invitation (pages 121–122)
- reminder notes (pages 123–124)
- take-home letter (pages 125–126)

Note: It is a good idea to send the workshop invitation home to families at least one week prior to the event. Then send the reminder note home at least three days prior to the event.

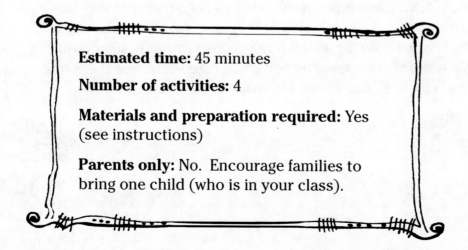

Estimated time: 45 minutes

Number of activities: 4

Materials and preparation required: Yes (see instructions)

Parents only: No. Encourage families to bring one child (who is in your class).

Phonemic Awareness Workshop

Agenda

Welcome/Introductions (5–10 minutes)

What Is Phonemic Awareness? (5 minutes)

Activity 1: Sing a Rhyming Song (10 minutes)

Activity 2: Clapping Syllables (5 minutes)

Activity 3: Beginning Sound Isolation (5 minutes)

Activity 4: Sound Hunt (5 minutes)

Questions/Share Ideas (5 minutes)

Welcome

Begin by welcoming families and allowing time for families to introduce themselves to one another. You may even want to provide snacks for participants.

What Is Phonemic Awareness?

Keep this section of the workshop brief, since children will be there and you don't want to lose their attention. Take just a few minutes to explain what phonemic awareness is and why it is a necessary step in the process of learning to read. You can use the script below to help you.

Note: You may want to make arrangements for another teacher or volunteer to take the children to another room or area for a short time to minimize distractions.

The focus of this workshop is phonemic awareness. When we think about learning to read, we typically think about learning phonics skills. In other words, we think about teaching children their letters and sounds. However, there is a step that is often overlooked, and that is phonemic awareness. Phonemic awareness refers to the identification of sounds in spoken language. Children must first recognize that the words that come out of their mouths are made up of individual sounds before we begin to teach them letters that represent those sounds. For example, by using phonics, we would say that the word cat *begins with the letter* C, *but with phonemic awareness, we would say that the word* cat *begins*

with the /k/ sound. The emphasis is on the sound rather than the letter. In this workshop, I'm going to show you several fun phonemic awareness games that you can play with your children and we'll try them out right here with your children.

Note: If children were out of the room for the above section, now is the time to bring them back in.

Activity 1: Sing a Rhyming Song

Explain that part of phonemic awareness is recognizing rhyming words. This can easily be practiced by singing rhyming songs. Begin by asking the parents and children to sing a familiar song along with you, such as "Twinkle, Twinkle, Little Star." Each time you come to a rhyming word, don't sing it, but let the parents and children fill it in. For example:

"Twinkle, Twinkle, Little Star"

How I wonder what you _____ (parents and kids sing "are")

Up above the world so high

Like a diamond in the _____ (parents and kids sing "sky")

Twinkle, Twinkle, Little Star

How I wonder what you _____ (parents and kids sing "are")

Explain to families that they don't need to tell children that they are singing rhyming words. This activity helps children recognize that our spoken language is made up of sounds. Provide families with ideas for other rhyming songs they know. Then have two or three adults form a group with their children to sing one of the songs together, leaving out the rhyming words for children to fill in. See below for rhyming song ideas.

Rhyming Song Ideas

"Itsy Bitsy Spider"

The itsy bitsy spider went up the waterspout.

Down came the rain and washed the spider out.

Out came the sun and dried up all the rain.

And the itsy bitsy spider went up the spout again.

"A-Hunting We Will Go"

Oh, a-hunting we will go, a-hunting we will go,

We'll take a little fox and put it in a box,

And then we'll let it go!

Oh, a-hunting we will go, a-hunting we will go,

We'll take a little snake and put it in a lake,

And then we'll let it go!

Oh, a-hunting we will go, a-hunting we will go,

We'll take a little cat and put it in a hat,

And then we'll let it go!

Nursery Rhyme Ideas

"Humpty Dumpty"

"Hickory, Dickory Dock"

"Mary Had a Little Lamb"

Activity 2: Clapping Syllables

Explain to parents that recognizing the number of syllables or beats in a word is another form of phonemic awareness. Show them how they can clap the beats in someone's name. For example, *Alexander* has four beats. The name *Ana* has two beats. Allow time for each parent to try clapping the names of people they know and counting the number of beats in each word.

Activity 3: Beginning Sound Isolation

Explain to parents that an important part of phonemic awareness is to recognize the sounds (not the letters) in words. An easy activity families can do is to name a word and ask what sound the child hears at the beginning of the word. Point out that it may be necessary to overemphasize the beginning sound so that children's attention is drawn to that sound. Have two or three parents form a group with their children to try out beginning-sound identification.

Activity 4: Sound Hunt

Share with parents a fun phonemic-awareness game that they can play at home or even riding in a car. To play, the parent selects a letter sound and asks the child to identify objects or people that begin with that sound. For example, the parent could say, "Let's find things that begin with the /b/ sound." Then the parent and child could look for things like a baby, a ball, a building, etc. Allow parents to try this activity with their children, looking for things that begin with a selected sound. Emphasize the hunt for sounds rather than letters.

Questions/Share Ideas

After completing the activities, allow a few minutes for parents to "debrief," sharing their thoughts, ideas, and questions. Ask them how they might include phonemic awareness activities into their daily lives at home. Encourage them to maintain a playlike environment when practicing phonemic awareness. The point is to have fun while enhancing literacy development.

Take-Home Letter

Finally, distribute copies of the Phonemic Awareness Take-Home Letter to parents. Explain that this letter will remind them of a few things they learned in the workshop and offers a few more suggestions for practicing phonemic awareness at home.

Note: If you plan to send home the phonemic awareness take-home letters found on pages 125–126 and on the Teacher Resource CD, mention this to parents so they can expect more ideas in future weeks.

Phonemic Awareness Workshop

Dear Family,

Please join us for a workshop about how children learn about the sounds of language. We will discuss how the recognition of sounds leads to reading success. You will leave this workshop with great ideas to use with your child at home. I hope you'll join us!

Your child is welcome to come!

Date: _____

Time: _____

Location: _____

Please let us know if you plan to come:

Contact: _____

Phone/Email: _____

Sincerely,

_____

Taller de la conciencia fonética

Phonemic Awareness Workshop

Querida familia:

Por favor venga a participar en un taller acerca de cómo los niños aprenden sobre los sonidos del lenguaje. Hablaremos de cómo el reconocimiento de los sonidos conduce al éxito en la lectura. Usted dejará este taller con buenas ideas que puede usar con su hijo en el hogar. ¡Espero que venga! ¡Su hijo también es bienvenido!

Fecha: _____

Hora: _____

Lugar: _____

Avísenos si piensa venir:

Contacto: _____

Número de teléfono/Correo electrónico:_____

Sinceramente,

_____

Don't Forget!

Don't forget, we're having a Phonemic Awareness Workshop! Come join us to learn about fun ways you can help your child achieve reading success.

Date: _____

Time: _____

Location: _____

Don't Forget!

Don't forget, we're having a Phonemic Awareness Workshop! Come join us to learn about fun ways you can help your child achieve reading success.

Date: _____

Time: _____

Location: _____

Don't Forget!

Don't forget, we're having a Phonemic Awareness Workshop! Come join us to learn about fun ways you can help your child achieve reading success.

Date: _____

Time: _____

Location: _____

Don't Forget!

Don't forget, we're having a Phonemic Awareness Workshop! Come join us to learn about fun ways you can help your child achieve reading success.

Date: _____

Time: _____

Location: _____

¡No se olvide!

No se olvide del taller de conciencia fonética. Venga a participar y aprender sobre divertidas maneras en que usted puede ayudar a que su hijo logre el éxito en la lectura.

Fecha: _____

Hora: _____

Lugar: _____

¡No se olvide!

No se olvide del taller de conciencia fonética. Venga a participar y aprender sobre divertidas maneras en que usted puede ayudar a que su hijo logre el éxito en la lectura.

Fecha: _____

Hora: _____

Lugar: _____

¡No se olvide!

No se olvide del taller de conciencia fonética. Venga a participar y aprender sobre divertidas maneras en que usted puede ayudar a que su hijo logre el éxito en la lectura.

Fecha: _____

Hora: _____

Lugar: _____

¡No se olvide!

No se olvide del taller de conciencia fonética. Venga a participar y aprender sobre divertidas maneras en que usted puede ayudar a que su hijo logre el éxito en la lectura.

Fecha: _____

Hora: _____

Lugar: _____

 #50753—An Educator's Guide to Family Involvement in Early Literacy

Phonemic Awareness Workshop Take-Home Letter

Dear Family,

Thank you for joining us for the Phonemic Awareness Workshop. I hope you were able to learn some fun activities that will draw your child's attention to the sounds in spoken language. Remember that phonemic awareness refers to the recognition of sounds in spoken language. Children must realize that the words they speak are made up of individual sounds before they can understand the purpose of learning letters that represent those sounds. As you focus on phonemic awareness in the coming weeks and months, try some of these additional activities:

- Sing rhyming songs with your child and have him or her add in the rhyming words.
- Read poetry to your child and emphasize the rhyming words.
- Listen for sounds in the environment. What sound does a bird make? What sound does a train make?
- Read rhyming books to your child. Many Dr. Seuss books have rhyming text.
- Clap the syllables (or beats) in the names of people you know.
- Look for objects in the community that begin with particular sounds.
- For a challenge, say all of the sounds of a word and see if your child can identify the word. For example, say /t//r//u//k/ and encourage your child to put the sounds together for the word *truck*.

By playing these fun and motivating games, you are helping your child to develop the necessary skills he or she will need for reading success!

Sincerely,

_____

Carta para llevar a casa sobre la conciencia fonética

Phonemic Awareness Workshop Take-Home Letter

Querida familia:

Gracias por participar en el taller de la conciencia fonética. Espero que haya podido aprender algunas actividades divertidas que hagan que su hijo sea consciente de los sonidos en el lenguaje hablado. Recuerde que la conciencia fonética se refiere al reconocimiento de los sonidos en un idioma hablado. Los niños deben darse cuenta de que las palabras que hablan están compuestas de sonidos individuales antes de que puedan entender el propósito de aprender las letras que esos sonidos representan. Mientras usted se enfoca en la conciencia fonética en las semanas y los meses que vienen, trate de hacer algunas de estas actividades adicionales.

- Cante con su hijo canciones que riman y haga que él o ella cante las palabras que riman.
- Leale poesía a su hijo y subraye la importancia de las palabras que riman.
- Trate de escuchar los sonidos de su entorno. ¿Qué sonido hace un ave? ¿Qué sonido hace un tren?
- Leale libros con rimas a su hijo. Muchos libros de Dr. Seuss tienen texto que rima.
- Dé palmadas con las sílabas (o al tiempo) en los nombres de la gente que conocen.
- Busque objetos en la comunidad que empiecen con sonidos particulares.
- Como reto, diga todos los sonidos de una palabra y vea si su hijo puede identificar la palabra. Por ejemplo, diga /t/ /r/ /u/ /k/ y anime a su hijo a juntar los sonidos para la palabra *truck*.

Al jugar estos juegos divertidos y motivadores, ¡usted está ayudando a que su hijo desarrolle las habilidades necesarias que necesitará para tener éxito en la lectura!

Sinceramente,

Read-Aloud Workshop

According to studies by the National Early Literacy Panel (NICHD 2000), there are interventions that are shown to be precursors for development of literacy skills. Two of the five identified interventions are shared reading experiences and parent programs. Shared reading refers to the practice of reading aloud to a child. Furthermore, it involves adult-child interaction and discussion during read-aloud experiences. Parent programs are described as providing techniques to parents that they can use with their children.

Because reading aloud to children is so important in the process of learning to read, it makes sense to conduct a workshop for parents explaining how they can have positive read-aloud experiences. You can also use the workshop as a way of promoting your favorite children's book author(s) and your favorite children's books.

The Read-Aloud Workshop includes the following:

- an agenda (page 128)
- detailed instructions and a script (pages 128–130)
- an invitation (pages 131–132)
- reminder notes (pages 133–134)
- take-home letter (pages 135–136)
- shared reading chart (page 137)

Note: It is a good idea to send the workshop invitation home to families at least one week prior to the event. Then send the reminder note home at least three days prior to the event.

Estimated time: 50–60 minutes

Number of activities: 3

Materials and preparation required: Yes (see instructions)

Parents only: No. Each parent should bring one young child.

Read-Aloud Workshop

Agenda

Welcome/Introductions (5–10 minutes)

Why Read Aloud to Your Child? (5 minutes)

Activity 1: Dialogic Reading (10–15 minutes)

Activity 2: Fluency Practice (10–15 minutes)

Activity 3: Track Reading Progress (10 minutes)

Questions/Share Ideas (5 minutes)

Welcome

Begin by welcoming families and allowing time for them to introduce themselves to one another. You may even want to provide snacks for participants.

Why Read Aloud to Your Child?

Take a few minutes to explain to parents why reading aloud to children is important. Include benefits of reading aloud and how it leads to the development of literacy skills. Also, mention the idea of dialogic reading, which will be explained in further detail. Feel free to use the script below to assist you with this portion of the workshop.

Note: You may want to make arrangements for another teacher or volunteer to take the children to another room or area for a short time to minimize distractions.

> *Thank you for attending this workshop about reading aloud to your child. Reading aloud to children is one of the things that leads to the development of early reading skills. Taking just a few minutes each day to read aloud to your child has an amazing impact. The National Early Literacy Panel has identified reading aloud as one of the best things parents can do to assist their children in becoming successful readers. During this workshop, I'm going to share with you a few ideas for reading aloud to your child. Hopefully, these ideas will motivate you to engage in daily read-aloud activities with your child.*

Activity 1: Dialogic Reading

Explain to families that there is more to reading aloud than just reading. Tell them that reading aloud is often called *shared reading*. It suggests that the experience is shared by both the reader and the listener. This process is also referred to as "dialogic reading," which suggests dialog or conversation. Explain to families that while reading to their children, they should feel free to talk to them, pointing out things in the illustrations and asking questions about what might happen next. Tell them that they will now have the opportunity to participate in shared reading and practice involving dialog in the reading process. Provide an assortment of books appropriate for the ages of the children in attendance. Allow families to select their books and then go back to their seats to read them together.

Activity 2: Fluency Practice

For the second activity, address the concept of fluency with families. Explain that fluency refers to the process of reading with accuracy, appropriate reading rate, and expression. Tell them that one of the best things for fluency development is for children to hear proper fluency. Mention that children's books often have wonderful characters whose voices and dialog lend themselves to the telling of the story. We can have all kinds of fun reading aloud to children when we emphasize the expressions of the characters. Briefly demonstrate reading with and without expression to point out the difference in interest. Provide an assortment of books that lend themselves to expressive reading and allow each family to select one. Then allow time for adults to read to their children using expression.

Activity 3: Track Reading Progress

For the final activity, explain to families that making time for reading aloud together can sometimes be difficult. Family life is busy, and we have schedules that sometimes keep us from doing what is important. Tell them that this activity will provide them with a way to track their daily reading progress. If family members in attendance are not reading aloud to their children every day, that's okay. Encourage them to increase gradually so that they will build a lasting habit. For example, if a family member currently reads to the child three days a week, that family member might want to set a goal to read four days a week and gradually increase to five, six, or (ideally) seven days a week. Provide each family with a few copies of the reading chart on page 137, or send a new chart home with children every month.

Questions/Share Ideas

After completing the activities, allow a few minutes for parents to "debrief," sharing their thoughts, ideas, and questions. Ask them how they might include shared reading experiences in their daily lives at home. As a final note, tell parents that children of all ages benefit from hearing stories read aloud to them. Often when children begin to read, parents are tempted to stop reading to their children in exchange for having the children read aloud to them. While having a child read aloud is certainly a good thing, don't let this take the place of the valuable and enjoyable experience of reading to the child.

Take-Home Letter

Finally, distribute copies of the Read-Aloud Take-Home Letter to parents. Explain that this letter will remind them of a few things they learned in the workshop and offers more suggestions for engaging in read-alouds at home.

Note: If you plan to send home the read-aloud take-home letters found on pages 135–136 and on the Teacher Resource CD, mention this to parents so they can expect more ideas in future weeks.

Read-Aloud Workshop

Dear Family,

Please join us for a fun workshop about reading aloud to your child. Children are invited! Bring one young child with you to try out different read-aloud strategies and learn about great children's books to read to your child.

Your child is welcome to come!

Date: _____

Time: _____

Location: _____

Please let us know if you plan to come:

Contact: _____

Phone/Email: _____

Sincerely,

_____

Taller de la lectura en voz alta

Read-Aloud Workshop

Querida familia:

Por favor venga a participar en un taller divertido sobre la lectura en voz alta. ¡Los niños están invitados! Traiga con usted a un hijo pequeño para intentar estrategias distintas de la lectura en voz alta y aprenda sobre buenos libros para los niños que pueda leerle a su hijo.

Fecha: _____

Hora: _____

Locación: _____

Avísenos si piensa venir:

Contacto: _____

Número de teléfono/Correo electrónico:

_____

Sinceramente,

_____

Don't Forget!

Don't forget, we're having a read-aloud workshop! Come join us to learn about fun ways you can enhance your child's beginning reading skills by reading stories. Be sure to bring your child with you.

Date: _____

Time: _____

Location: _____

Don't Forget!

Don't forget, we're having a read-aloud workshop! Come join us to learn about fun ways you can enhance your child's beginning reading skills by reading stories. Be sure to bring your child with you.

Date: _____

Time: _____

Location: _____

Don't Forget!

Don't forget, we're having a read-aloud workshop! Come join us to learn about fun ways you can enhance your child's beginning reading skills by reading stories. Be sure to bring your child with you.

Date: _____

Time: _____

Location: _____

Don't Forget!

Don't forget, we're having a read-aloud workshop! Come join us to learn about fun ways you can enhance your child's beginning reading skills by reading stories. Be sure to bring your child with you.

Date: _____

Time: _____

Location: _____

¡No se olvide!

No se olvide del taller de lectura en voz alta. Venga a participar y aprender sobre divertidas maneras para aumentar las primeras habilidades de lectura al leer cuentos. Asegúrese de traer a su hijo con usted.

Fecha: _____

Hora: _____

Locacíon: _____

- -

¡No se olvide!

No se olvide del taller de lectura en voz alta. Venga a participar y aprender sobre divertidas maneras para aumentar las primeras habilidades de lectura al leer cuentos. Asegúrese de traer a su hijo con usted.

Fecha: _____

Hora: _____

Locacíon: _____

- -

¡No se olvide!

No se olvide del taller de lectura en voz alta. Venga a participar y aprender sobre divertidas maneras para aumentar las primeras habilidades de lectura al leer cuentos. Asegúrese de traer a su hijo con usted.

Fecha: _____

Hora: _____

Locacíon: _____

- -

¡No se olvide!

No se olvide del taller de lectura en voz alta. Venga a participar y aprender sobre divertidas maneras para aumentar las primeras habilidades de lectura al leer cuentos. Asegúrese de traer a su hijo con usted.

Fecha: _____

Hora: _____

Locacíon: _____

Read-Aloud Workshop Take-Home Letter

Dear Family,

Thank you for joining us for the workshop about reading aloud to your child. I hope you were able to learn a few new things and that you had an enjoyable time reading with your child. Remember that reading aloud to your child greatly increases the development of his or her literacy skills. All it takes is a few minutes each day to positively affect your child. Here are a few concepts we discussed at the workshop:

Dialogic Reading: This refers to having dialog or conversation while reading aloud to a child. Be sure to point out illustrations and ask your child questions about the story as you read.

Fluency: This involves reading with accuracy, appropriate rate, and expression. As you read to your child, have fun reading with expression and imagining how the characters in the story might speak.

More Activities to Try:

- Go to the library and select books together.
- Keep a list of favorite authors and look for their books at the library and at bookstores.
- After reading a book to your child, act out parts of the story together.
- Ask your child to tell you how he or she thinks certain characters feel about what happens in the story.
- Ask your child to talk about experiences he or she may have had that relate to events in the story.
- Be sure to read the same books over and over again to your child. Children often love to hear stories more than once.

Sincerely,

_____

Carta para llevar a casa sobre la lectura en voz alta

Read-Aloud Workshop Take-Home Letter

Querida familia:

Gracias por participar en el taller sobre la lectura en voz alta a su hijo. Espero que haya podido aprender unas cosas nuevas y que haya disfrutado leyendo con su hijo. Recuerde que la lectura en voz alta con su hijo aumenta en gran manera el desarrollo de sus habilidades de la lectoescritura. Sólo toma unos pocos minutos cada día para influenciar positivamente a su hijo. Aquí hay unos conceptos que discutimos en el taller:

La lectura dialogística: Esto se refiere a tener un diálogo o conversación mientras le lee en voz alta a su hijo. Asegúrese de señalar las ilustraciones y hágale preguntas a su hijo sobre el cuento mientras le lee.

La fluidez: Esto involucra la lectura con precisión, ritmo apropiado y expresión. Mientras le lee a su hijo, diviértase leyendo con expresión e imagine cómo podrían hablar los personajes en el cuento.

Más actividades para intentar:

- Vaya a la biblioteca y seleccionen libros juntos.
- Mantenga una lista de autores favoritos y busque sus libros en la biblioteca y en las librerías.
- Después de leerle un libro a su hijo, representen partes del cuento juntos.
- Pídale a su hijo que le diga cómo él o ella piensa que ciertos personajes se sienten sobre lo que sucede en el cuento.
- Pídale a su hijo que hable sobre las experiencias que quizás haya tenido que se relacionan a los eventos del cuento.
- Asegúrese de leer los mismos libros una y otra vez a su hijo. Los niños a menudo disfrutan de escuchar los cuentos más de una vez.

Sinceramente,

_____

 #50753—An Educator's Guide to Family Involvement in Early Literacy

Shared Reading Chart

Make a check (√) in a small box to indicate your plan to read aloud to your child on a particular day. Draw an X in a large box on a day you actually read aloud together.

Month:	Sunday	Monday	Tuesday	Wednesday	Thursday	Friday	Saturday

Let's Get Cooking Workshop

Cooking together is a great way for families and children to engage in conversation while emphasizing academic skills. Cooking often involves mathematics and literacy skills. By offering this workshop to parents, you can point out the educational benefits of cooking together.

The Let's Get Cooking workshop includes the following:

- an agenda (page 139)
- detailed instructions and a script (pages 139–141)
- an invitation (pages 142–143)
- reminder notes (pages 144–145)
- take-home letter (pages 146–147)

Note: It is a good idea to send the workshop invitation home to families at least one week prior to the event. Then send the reminder note home at least three days prior to the event.

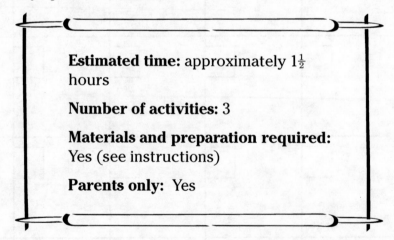

Estimated time: approximately $1\frac{1}{2}$ hours

Number of activities: 3

Materials and preparation required: Yes (see instructions)

Parents only: Yes

Let's Get Cooking Workshop

Agenda

Welcome/Introductions (5–10 minutes)

The Academic Benefits of Cooking with Your Child (5 minutes)

Activity 1: Tastefully Topped English Muffins (10 minutes)

Activity 2: Pleasing Pizza (20 minutes)

Activity 3: Yogurt and Toppings (10 minutes)

Questions/Share Ideas (5 minutes)

Welcome

Begin by welcoming families and allowing time for them to introduce themselves to one another. You may even want to provide snacks for participants.

The Academic Benefits of Cooking with Your Child

Take a few minutes to explain to families how cooking with their children can lead to academic benefits. Mention that, through cooking, they can model literacy skills, such as reading a cookbook or recipe card. They can also model how to make a grocery list of items needed for a particular meal. While cooking, they can discuss mathematical concepts, such as measurement, fractions, counting, etc. Use the script below, if desired.

Thank you for attending this workshop about cooking with your child. It's amazing, but something as common as cooking at home with your child is a great way to support academic learning and communicate to your child that reading, writing, and math skills are meaningful and purposeful parts of our daily lives. Through cooking, you can model the purpose of reading by reading recipe instructions out of cookbooks or from recipe cards. You can model the purpose of writing by listing the food items needed to create a particular recipe. While you and your child are cooking, you can mention mathematical concepts, such as measuring two tablespoons of peanut butter or needing to use half an apple. Cooking is a great way to stimulate your child's interest in many important skills.

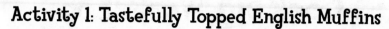

Activity 1: Tastefully Topped English Muffins

Explain to parents that for this recipe, they will simply top an English muffin with some kind of spread, such as peanut butter, cottage cheese, ricotta cheese, or jelly. Then they will add nutritious toppings, such as raisins, nuts, or fruit slices. Provide these food items for parents and allow them to make a muffin creation to eat before continuing on with a discussion about this recipe. When parents are seated and enjoying their muffins, ask them to think about the ways they could draw attention to reading, writing, or mathematical concepts. Point out that a parent could list the ingredients and ask the child to read the ingredients with assistance. A parent could model the writing of the list of ingredients. While assembling the Tastefully Topped English Muffin, a parent could ask the child to measure two tablespoons of cottage cheese and place eight raisins and two grapes on top. Encourage parents to discuss other ways they might support academic learning.

Activity 2: Pleasing Pizza

For the second activity, introduce making personal pizzas. For this activity, you will need to provide individual-sized precooked pizza crusts, pizza sauce, shredded cheese, and an assortment of toppings. Also, have a microwave oven or a toaster oven available. Allow time for families to assemble their pizza slices and warm them up. While they are eating, ask them to think about the possible academic skills that could be brought up with their children while making Pleasing Pizzas. Be sure to point out that children could talk about putting sauce and cheese on the *whole* pizza, but only putting pepperoni on *half*. They could also have their children place a certain number of mushrooms or olives on top.

Activity 3: Yogurt and Toppings

For the final activity, explain to families that they will make a healthy dessert. They should scoop some flavored yogurt (or pudding) into a bowl and then add various toppings, such as graham cracker crumbs, raisins, or strawberry slices. Point out that a familiy member could provide measuring cups and spoons for the child to measure $\frac{1}{4}$ cup of yogurt and 1 tablespoon of graham cracker crumbs, etc. Invite families to make suggestions for how they could use this activity to create literacy connections.

Questions/Share Ideas

After completing the activities, allow a few minutes for parents to "debrief," sharing their thoughts, ideas, and questions. Ask them how they might provide other cooking experiences for their children at home. Also, encourage them to think about cooking tasks that they would need to do for their children for the sake of safety.

Take-Home Letter

Finally, distribute copies of the Let's Get Cooking Take-Home Letter to parents. Explain that this letter will remind them of a few things that they learned in the workshop and offers a few more suggestions for reinforcing academic skills through cooking at home.

Note: If you plan to send home the Let's Get Cooking Take-Home letters found on pages 146–147 and on the Teacher Resource CD, mention this to parents so they can expect more ideas in future weeks.

Let's Get Cooking Workshop

Dear Family,

Please join us for a fun workshop about cooking with your child. You will learn about the educational benefits of cooking with your child and leave with several fun activities that you can try at home. This workshop is for parents or other adults only. No children, please.

Date: _____

Time: _____

Location: _____

Please let us know if you plan to come:

Contact: _____

Phone/Email: _____

Sincerely,

_____

Taller de cocinar para los niños

Let's Get Cooking Workshop

Querida familia:

Por favor venga a participar en un taller divertido sobre cocinar con su hijo. Aprenderán sobre los beneficios educativos de cocinar con su hijo y dejará el taller con varias actividades divertidas que puede intentar en el hogar. Este taller es solamente para los adultos, por favor.

Fecha: _____

Hora: _____

Locación: _____

Avísenos si piensa venir:

Contacto: _____

Número de teléfono/Correo electrónico:

_____

Sinceramente,

_____

Family Literacy Workshops

Don't Forget!

Don't forget, we're having a cooking workshop! Come join us to learn about fun ways you can support your child's academic development through cooking. No children, please!

Date: _____

Time: _____

Location: _____

Don't Forget!

Don't forget, we're having a cooking workshop! Come join us to learn about fun ways you can support your child's academic development through cooking. No children, please!

Date: _____

Time: _____

Location: _____

Don't Forget!

Don't forget, we're having a cooking workshop! Come join us to learn about fun ways you can support your child's academic development through cooking. No children, please!

Date: _____

Time: _____

Location: _____

Don't Forget!

Don't forget, we're having a cooking workshop! Come join us to learn about fun ways you can support your child's academic development through cooking. No children, please!

Date: _____

Time: _____

Location: _____

¡No se olvide!

No se olvide del taller de cocinar. Venga a participar y aprender sobre divertidas maneras para apoyar el desarrollo académico de su hijo a través de la cocina. ¡Sólo para los adultos!

Fecha: _____

Hora: _____

Lugar: _____

¡No se olvide!

No se olvide del taller de cocinar. Venga a participar y aprender sobre divertidas maneras para apoyar el desarrollo académico de su hijo a través de la cocina. ¡Sólo para los adultos!

Fecha: _____

Hora: _____

Lugar: _____

¡No se olvide!

No se olvide del taller de cocinar. Venga a participar y aprender sobre divertidas maneras para apoyar el desarrollo académico de su hijo a través de la cocina. ¡Sólo para los adultos!

Fecha: _____

Hora: _____

Lugar: _____

¡No se olvide!

No se olvide del taller de cocinar. Venga a participar y aprender sobre divertidas maneras para apoyar el desarrollo académico de su hijo a través de la cocina. ¡Sólo para los adultos!

Fecha: _____

Hora: _____

Lugar: _____

Let's Get Cooking Workshop Take-Home Letter

Dear Family,

Thank you for joining us for the Let's Get Cooking Workshop. I hope that you learned a few new things about the academic benefits of cooking with your child. Remember that cooking with your child at home reinforces reading, writing, and mathematical skills in a very natural way.

In the future, you may want to read some books about food to go along with your cooking adventures. See the list below for fun children's books about food.

Bread and Jam for Frances by Russell Hoban

Chicken Soup with Rice by Maurice Sendak

Cloudy with a Chance of Meatballs by Judi Barrett

Eating the Alphabet: Fruits and Vegetables from A to Z by Lois Elhert

Green Eggs and Ham by Dr. Seuss

Sun Bread by Elisa Kleven

Today Is Monday by Eric Carle

Walter the Baker by Eric Carle

Don't forget to try those great recipes for:

- Tastefully Topped English Muffins

- Pleasing Pizza

- Yogurt and Toppings

Sincerely,

_____

Carta para llevar a casa sobre un taller de cocinar

Let's Get Cooking Workshop Take-Home Letter

Querida familia:

Gracias por participar en el taller sobre cocinar con su hijo. Espero que haya aprendido unas cosas nuevas sobre los beneficios académicos de cocinar con su hijo. Recuerde que cocinar con su hijo en el hogar refuerza la lectura, la escritura y las destrezas matemáticas en una manera natural.

En el futuro, quizás querrá leer unos libros sobre la comida que acompañarán sus aventuras en la cocina. Vea la lista con libros divertidos para niños sobre la comida.

Today Is Monday by Eric Carle

Chicken Soup with Rice by Maurice Sendak

Sun Bread by Elisa Kleven

Walter the Baker by Eric Carle

Cloudy with a Chance of Meatballs by Judi Barrett

Green Eggs and Ham by Dr. Seuss

Bread and Jam for Frances by Russell Hoban

Eating the Alphabet: Fruits and Vegetables from A to Z by Lois Elhert

No olvide intentar estas buenas recetas para:

- Tastefully Topped English Muffins
- Pleasing Pizza
- Yogurt and Toppings

Sinceramente,

_____

Notes

Conclusion

There's something in their eyes
There's something in their hearts
There's something in their souls
That longs to hear a story.

—Steven L. Layne

Teacher-Family Partnerships

The benefits of family involvement in early literacy development are clearly worth the time and effort involved in planning opportunities and working to develop teacher-family partnerships. As you begin the rewarding process of forming partnerships with families, it is necessary to remember the following important points:

- The benefits of family involvement extend to children, families, and teachers.

- Children learn many important things about literacy from their home environments. As teachers, we must recognize and value the literacy contributions of families.

- Family involvement can take on many forms. Most important is family involvement that takes place in the home. Inviting parents to assist in classroom-based activities can also help build connections between schools and families.

- An important focus of family involvement relates to the formation of teacher-family partnerships. Teachers can implement ways to reach out to parents to establish lines of communication in order to work together for the benefit of children.

- Involving parents in the classroom is a great way to connect parents to the activities taking place at school. Teachers can create and offer opportunities for parents to volunteer in the classroom.

- Recognizing that the greatest benefits of parent involvement result when that involvement takes place in the home, teachers can offer creative ideas for families to engage in educational support of their children at home.

- Finally, families can benefit from periodic workshops that allow them to learn more about involving themselves in their children's education while interacting with you and other parents.

Empowering Families

As teachers, we must keep in mind that the greatest thing we can do to encourage family involvement is to empower parents. "It is our role as the teacher to demonstrate for parents how much power and influence they exert in the academic success of their children. It is our responsibility as the teacher to express to parents their value in the educational process" (Prior and Gerard 2007, 22). In his Ecological Systems Theory, Bronfenbrenner (1979) emphasizes that the family has the most impact on the child. For this reason, empowering parents is a necessary part of a child's education. The environment a teacher creates must be supportive of children and their families (Swick 2003).

Decades of research point to the conclusion that the benefits of family involvement are extensive and have even greater long-terms benefits when begun in the early years. As early childhood educators, we have the responsibility to involve parents in the educational process if we hope to adequately address each child's educational needs to the fullest.

References Cited

Anderson, G., and Markle, A. 1985. Cheerios, McDonald's and Snickers: Bringing EP into the classroom. *Reading Education in Texas* 1: 30–35.

Anderson, R. C., E. H. Hiebert, J. A. Scott, and I. A. G. Wilkinson. 1985. *Becoming a nation of readers: The report of the Commission on Reading.* Champaign, IL: Centre for the Study of Reading.

Bergen, D. and D. Mauer. 2000. Symbolic play, phonological awareness, and literacy skills at three age levels. In *Play and literacy in early childhood: Research from multiple perspectives*, ed. K. Roskos and J. F. Christie, 45–62. Mahwah, NJ; London: Earlbaum.

Bronfenbrenner, U. 1979. *The ecology of human development.* Cambridge, MA: Harvard University Press.

Carter, S. 2002. *The impact of parent/family involvement on student outcomes: An annotated bibliography of research from the past decade.* Eugene, OR: Consortium for Appropriate Dispute Resolution in Special Education. Washington DC.

Center for the Improvement of Early Reading Achievement (CIERA). 2001a. *Put reading first: The research building blocks for teaching children to read.* The Partnership for Reading: National Institute for Literacy; National Institute of Child Health and Human Development; and U.S. Department of Education. Washington DC.

———. 2001b. *Put reading first: Helping your child learn to read.* The Partnership for Reading: National Institute for Literacy; National Institute of Child Health and Human Development; and U.S. Department of Education. Washington DC.

Christenson, S. L. 1995. Families and schools: What is the role of the school psychologist? School Psychology Quarterly 10(2): 118–132.

Christie, J. F., J. B. Enz, M. R. Gerard, M. Han, and J. Prior. April 2003, *Examining the instructional uses of environmental print.* Paper presented at the 48th Annual Convention of the International Reading Association, Orlando, FL.

Christie, J. F., J. B. Enz, and C. Vukelich. 2002. *Teaching language and literacy: Preschool through the elementary grades.* New York: Longman.

Clark, M. M. 1984. Literacy at home and at school: Insights from a study of young fluent readers. In *Awakening to literacy* H. Goelman, A. Oberg, and F. Smith eds.,(122–130). Portsmouth, NJ: Heinemann.

Elkind, D. 1990. *The child and society: Essays in applied child development.* New York: Oxford University Press.

Epstein, J. L. 1983. *Effects on parents of teacher practices in parent involvement.* Baltimore, MD: Center on Families, Communities, Schools and Children's Learning, Johns Hopkins University.

———. 1984. School policy and parent involvement: Research results. *Educational Horizons* 62 (2): 70–72.

———. 2000. *School and family partnerships: Preparing educators and improving schools.* Boulder, CO: Westview.

Faires, J., W. D. Nichols, and R. J. Rickelman. 2000. *Effects of parent involvement in developing competent readers in first grade.* Reading Psychology 21: 195–215.

Faucette, E. Nov/Dec 2000. *Are you missing the most important ingredient? A recipe for increasing achievement.* Multimedia Schools 7(6): 56–61.

Foy, J. G., and V. Mann. 2003. Home literacy environment and phonological awareness in preschool children: Differential effects for rhyme and phoneme awareness. *Applied Psycholinguistics* 24: 59–88.

Goldberg, C. N. 1989. Making success a more common occurrence for children at risk for failure: Lessons from Hispanic first-graders learning to read. In *Risk makers, risk takers, risk breakers: Reducing the risks for young literacy learners,* ed. J. F. Allen and J. M. Mason, 48–79. Portsmouth, NH: Heinemann.

Harste, J., C. Burke, and V. Woodward. 1982. Children's language and world: Initial encounters with print. In *Reader meets author/bridging the gap: A psycholinguistic and sociolinguistic perspective,* ed. J.A. Langer and M.T. Smith Burke, 105–131. Newark, DE: International Reading Association.

Henderson, A. T., and N. Berla. 1994. *A new generation of evidence: The family is critical to student achievement.* St. Louis, MO: Danforth Foundation; Flint, MI: Mott (C.S.) Foundation.

Kreider, H. 2002. *Getting parents "ready" for kindergarten: The role of early childhood education.* Amherst, MA: Harvard Family Research Project. http://www.gse.Harvard.edu/hfrp/projects/fine/resources/research/kreider.html (accessed January 23, 2005).

Kuby, P., and J. Aldridge. 1997. Direct versus indirect environmental print instruction and early reading ability in kindergarten children. *Reading Psychology: International Quarterly* 18 (2): 91–104.

Miedel, W. T. and A. J. Reynolds. 1999. Parent involvement in early intervention for disadvantaged children: Does it matter? *Journal of School Psychology* 37 (4): 379–399.

Morrow, L. 1993. *Literacy development in the early years: Helping children read and write.* Boston, MA: Allyn and Bacon.

Moore, K.B. (2002). Family communications: Ideas that really work. *Early Childhood Today* 17 (2): 14–15.

Morrow, L. and Rand, M. 1991. Preparing the classroom environment to promote literacy behavior during play. In *Play and Early Literacy*, ed. J. Christie. New York: State University of New York Press.

National Institute of Child Health and Human Development (NICHD). 2000. *Report of the National Reading Panel: Teaching children to read: An evidence-based assessment of the scientific research literature on reading and its implications for reading instruction.* (NIH Publication No. 004769). Washington, DC: U.S. Government Printing Office.

Neuman, S. B. and K. Roskos. 1990. The influence of literacy-enriched play settings on preschoolers' engagement with written language. In *Literacy theory and research: Analyses from multiple paradigms*, ed. S. McCormick and J. Zutell, 179–187. Chicago, IL: National Reading Conference.

Park, H. 2008. Home literacy environments and children's reading performance: a comparative study of 25 countries. *Educational Research and Evaluation* 14 (6): 489–505.

Pellegrini, A. D., L. Galda, J. Dresden, and S. Cox. 1991. A longitudinal study of the predictive relations among symbolic play, linguistic verbs, and early literacy. *Research in the Teaching of English* 25: 219–235.

Prior, J. 2003. *Environmental print: Meaningful connections for learning to read.* Unpublished doctoral dissertation, Arizona State University, Tempe.

Prior, J. and M. R. Gerard. 2004. *Environmental print in the classroom: Meaningful connections for learning to read.* Newark: DE: International Reading Association.

———. 2007. *Family involvement in early childhood education: Research into practice.* Wadsworth Publishing.

Purcell-Gates, V. 1996. Stories, coupons and the *TV Guide*: Relationships between home literacy experiences and emergent literacy knowledge. *Reading Research Quarterly* 31: 406–428.

———. 2000. Family literacy. In *Handbook of reading research*, ed. M. L. Kamil, P. B. Mosenthal, P. D. Pearson, and R. Barr, Vol. 3, 853–870. Mahwah, NJ: Erlbaum.

Quigley, D. D. April 2000. *Parents and teachers working together to support third grade achievement: Parents as learning partners.* Paper presented at the annual meeting of the American Educational Research Association, New Orleans, LA.

Roskos, K. May 2000. Creating connections, building constructions: Language, literacy, and play in early childhood. In *Reading on line* [Online]. http://www.readingonline.org/articles/roskos/article.html.

Shaver, A. V and R. T Walls. 1998. Effect of Title I parent involvement on student reading and mathematics achievement. *Journal of Research and Development in Education* 31 (2): 90–97.

Swick, K. Summer 2003. Communication concepts for strengthening family-school-community partnerships. *Early Childhood Education Journal* 30 (4): 275–280.

Teale, W. 1984. Toward a theory of how children learn to read and write naturally. *Language Arts* 59: 555–570.

van Steensel, R. 2006. Relations between socio-cultural factors, the home literacy environment and children's literacy development in the first years of primary education. *Journal of Research in Reading* 29 (4): 367–382.

West, J. M. 2000. *Increasing parent involvement for student motivation.* Armidale, New South Wales, Australia: University of New England (ERIC Document Reproduction Service No. ED 448411).

Wobmann, L. 2003. Schooling resources, educational institutions, and student performance: The international evidence. *Oxford Bulletin of Economics and Statistics* 65: 117–170.

Yaden, D. B., D.W. Rowe, and L. MacGillivray. 2000. Emergent literacy: A matter (polyphony) of perspectives. In *Handbook of reading research*, ed. M. L. Kamil, P. B. Mosental, P. D. Pearson, and R. Barr, 425–454. Mahwah, NJ: Lawrence Erlbaum Associates.

Yopp, H. K., and R. H Yopp. 2000. Supporting phonemic awareness development in the classroom. *The Reading Teacher* 54: 130–143.

Recommended Children's Literature

Ahlberg, Allan. *The Jolly Postman or Other People's Letters*. Boston: Little, Brown, and Company, 1986.

Barrett, Judi. *Cloudy With a Chance of Meatballs*. New York: Atheneum, 1982.

Cannon, Janell. *Stellaluna*. New York: Harcourt, Inc., 1993.

———. *Pinduli*. New York: Harcourt Children's Books, 2004.

Carle, Eric. *Walter the Baker*. New York: Aladdin, 1998.

———. *Today Is Monday*. New York: Putnam Juvenile, 1997.

———. *The Grouchy Ladybug*. New York: HarperCollins, 1996.

———. *The Very Hungry Caterpillar*. New York: Penguin Group USA, 1986.

Elhert, Lois. *Eating the Alphabet: Fruits and Vegetables from A to Z*. New York: Houghton Mifflin, 1993.

Hoban, Russell. *Bread and Jam for Frances*. New York: HarperCollins, 2008.

Hoberman, Mary Ann. *Skip to My Lou*. New York: Megan Tingley, 2003.

———. *I Know an Old Lady Who Swallowed a Fly*. New York: Little, Brown Books for Young Readers, 1980.

Katz, Alan and David Catrow. *Are You Quite Polite?* New York: Margaret K. McElderry Books, 2006.

———. *Take Me Out of the Bathtub*. New York: Margaret K. McElderry Books, 2001.

Kleven, Elisa. *Sun Bread*. New York: Puffin, 2004.

Langstaff, John. *Oh, A-Hunting We Will Go*. New York: Aladdin, 1991.

———. *Over in the Meadow*. New York: Sandpiper, 1973.

Lobel, Arnold. *Frog and Toad Together*. New York: Harper Festival, 1999.

———. *Frog and Toad Are Friends*. New York: HarperCollins, 1970.

Martin Jr., Bill. *Brown Bear, Brown Bear, What Do You See?* New York: Henry Holt and Co., 1992.

Martin Jr., Bill, and John Archambault. *Chicka Chicka Boom Boom*. New York: Simon and Schuster, 1989.

McKissack, Patricia. *Mirandy and Brother Wind*. Oklahoma: Dragonfly Books, 1997.

Meyer, Mercer. *There's a Nightmare in My Closet*. New York: Puffin, 1992.

———. *What Do You Do With a Kangaroo?* New York: Scholastic, 1987.

Munsch, Robert. *50 Below Zero*. Canada: Annick Press, 1992.

———. *Love You Forever*. Canada: Firefly, 1987.

Numeroff, Laura. *If You Give a Moose a Muffin*. New York: Scholastic, 1991.

———. *If You Give a Mouse a Cookie*. New York: Scholastic, 1985.

Prelutsky, Jack. *Read a Rhyme, Write a Rhyme*. Oklahoma: Dragonfly Books, 2009.

———. *A Pizza the Size of the Sun*. New York: Greenwillow Books, 1996.

———. *Something Big Has Been Here*. New York: Greenwillow Books, 1990.

———. *Read-Aloud Rhymes for the Very Young*. New York: Knopf Books for Young Readers, 1986.

———. *The Random House Book of Poetry for Children*. New York: Random House, 1983.

Raffi. *Baby Beluga*. New York: Crown Books for Young Readers, 1992.

———. *Down by the Bay*. New York: Crown Books for Young Readers, 1988.

———. *Shake My Sillies Out*. New York: Crown Books for Young Readers, 1988.

Sendak, Maurice. *Chicken Soup with Rice*. New York: Scholastic, 1972.

Seuss, Dr. *Green Eggs and Ham*. New York: Random House Books for Young Readers, 1960.

Silverstein, Shel. *Falling Up*. New York: HarperCollins Publishers, 1996.

———. *A Light in the Attic*. New York: Harper and Row, 1981.

———. *Where the Sidewalk Ends*. New York: HarperCollins Publishers, 1974.

Soto, Gary. *If the Shoe Fits*. New York: Putnam Juvenile, 2002.

———. *Too Many Tamales*. Iowa: Perfection Learning, 1996.

Stevenson, Robert Louis. *A Child's Garden of Verses*. New York: Star Bright Books, 2008.

Viorst, Judith. *I'll Fix Anthony*. New York: Aladdin Picture Books, 1988.

———. *If I Were in Charge of the World (and Other Worries)*. New York: Antheneum, 1984.

———. *Alexander and the Terrible, Horrible, No Good, Very Bad Day*. New York: Simon and Schuster, 1972.

Westcott, Nadine Bernard. *Peanut Butter and Jelly: A Play Rhyme*. New York: Puffin. 1992.

———. *The Lady with the Alligator Purse*. New York: Little, Brown Books for Young Readers, 1990.

———. *Never Take a Pig to Lunch (and Other Poems about the Fun of Eating)*. New York: Orchard Books, 1988.

Willems, Mo. *The Pigeon Finds a Hot Dog!* New York: Hyperion Book CH, 2004.

———. *Don't Let the Pigeon Drive the Bus!* New York: Hyperion Press, 2003.

Wood, Audrey. *Silly Sally*. New York: Harcourt Children's Books, 1999.

———. *The Napping House*. New York: Scholastic, 1996.

Yolen, Jane. *Greyling*. New York: Philomel, 1991.

———. *Owl Moon*. New York: Philomel, 1987.

Contents of the Teacher Resource CD

Page	Template Name	Filename
NA	Thank-You Cards (English)	thankyou_eng.pdf; thankyou_eng.doc
NA	Thank-You Cards (Spanish)	thankyou_sp.pdf; thankyou_sp.doc
78	Journal Page	journal.pdf; journal.doc
79	Backpack Tracking Sheet	tracking.pdf; tracking.doc
137	Shared Reading Chart	readingchart.pdf; readingchart.doc

Page	Letter Title	Filename
17	Encouraging Literacy Development at Home (English)	literacyhome_eng.pdf; literacyhome_eng.doc
18	Encouraging Literacy Development at Home (Spanish)	literacyhome_sp.pdf; literacyhome_sp.doc
30	Job Sign-Up (English)	signup_eng.pdf; signup_eng.doc
31	Job Sign-Up (Spanish)	signup_sp.pdf; signup_sp.doc
35	Finger Puppets (English)	finger_eng.pdf; finger_eng.doc
36	Finger Puppets (Spanish)	finger_sp.pdf; finger_sp.doc
37	Paper-Bag Puppets (English)	paperbag_eng.pdf; paperbag_eng.doc
38	Paper-Bag Puppets (Spanish)	paperbag_sp.pdf; paperbag_sp.doc
39	Dramatizing Stories (English)	stories_eng.pdf; stories_eng.doc
40	Dramatizing Stories (Spanish)	stories_sp.pdf; stories_sp.doc
41	Asking Questions (English)	questions_eng.pdf; questions_eng.doc
42	Asking Questions (Spanish)	questions_sp.pdf; questions_sp.doc
44	Environmental Print Activities (English)	epactivities_eng.pdf; epactivities_eng.doc
45	Environmental Print Activities (Spanish)	epactivities_sp.pdf; epactivities_sp.doc
46	Interact with Environmental Print (English)	interact_eng.pdf; interact_eng.doc
47	Interact with Environmental Print (Spanish)	interact_sp.pdf; interact_sp.doc
48	Environmental Print at Home (English)	home_eng.pdf; home_eng.doc
49	Environmental Print at Home (Spanish)	home_sp.pdf; home_sp.doc
50	Fun with Environmental Print (English)	fun_eng.pdf; fun_eng.doc
51	Fun with Environmental Print (Spanish)	fun_sp.pdf; fun_sp.doc
52	Environmental Print Is Everywhere (English)	everywhere_eng.pdf; everywhere_eng.doc
53	Environmental Print Is Everywhere (Spanish)	everywhere_sp.pdf; everywhere_sp.doc
54	Environmental Print and Literacy (English)	literacy_eng.pdf; literacy_eng.doc
55	Environmental Print and Literacy (Spanish)	literacy_sp.pdf; literacy_sp.doc
60	Reading and Writing Fun Backpack (English)	readingandwriting_eng.pdf; readingandwriting_eng.doc
61	Reading and Writing Fun Backpack (Spanish)	readingandwriting_sp.pdf; readingandwriting_sp.doc
62	Counting On Reading Backpack (English)	countingon_eng.pdf; countingon_eng.doc
63	Counting On Reading Backpack (Spanish)	countingon_sp.pdf; countingon_sp.doc
64	Let's Write! Backpack (English)	letswrite_eng.pdf; letswrite_eng.doc
65	Let's Write! Backpack (Spanish)	letswrite_sp.pdf; letswrite_sp.doc
66	Read It! Make It! Backpack (English)	readitmakeit_eng.pdf; readitmakeit_eng.doc
67	Read It! Make It! Backpack (Spanish)	readitmakeit_sp.pdf; readitmakeit_sp.doc
68	Special Visitor Backpack (English)	visitor_eng.pdf; visitor_eng.doc
69	Special Visitor Backpack (Spanish)	visitor_sp.pdf; visitor_sp.doc
70	Let's Talk! Backpack (English)	talk_eng.pdf; talk_eng.doc
	Let's Talk! Backpack (Spanish)	talk_sp.pdf; talk_sp.doc
	Backpack (English)	makeit_eng.pdf; makeit_eng.doc
	(Spanish)	makeit_sp.pdf; makeit_sp.doc

Contents of the Teacher Resource CD

Page	Letter Title	Filename
74	Measuring Up! Backpack (English)	measuring_eng.pdf; measuring_eng.doc
75	Measuring Up! Backpack (Spanish)	measuring_sp.pdf; measuring_sp.doc
76	Making Music Backpack (English)	music_eng.pdf; music_eng.doc
77	Making Music Backpack (Spanish)	music_sp.pdf; music_sp.doc
80	Development of Early Reading Skills (English)	earlyreading_eng.pdf; earlyreading_eng.doc
81	Development of Early Reading Skills (Spanish)	earlyreading_sp.pdf; earlyreading_sp.doc
82	Development of Early Writing Skills (English)	earlywriting_eng.pdf; earlywriting_eng.doc
83	Development of Early Writing Skills (Spanish)	earlywriting_sp.pdf; earlywriting_sp.doc
84	Creating a Literacy-Rich Environment (English)	literacyrich_eng.pdf; literacyrich_eng.doc
85	Creating a Literacy-Rich Environment (Spanish)	literacyrich_sp.pdf; literacyrich_sp.doc
86	Let's Play! (English)	letsplay_eng.pdf; letsplay_eng.doc
87	Let's Play! (Spanish)	letsplay_sp.pdf; letsplay_sp.doc
88	Beginning, Middle, End (English)	begin_eng.pdf; begin_eng.doc
89	Beginning, Middle, End (Spanish)	begin_sp.pdf; begin_sp.doc
90	Great Authors (English)	greatauthors_eng.pdf; greatauthors_eng.doc
91	Great Authors (Spanish)	greatauthors_sp.pdf; greatauthors_sp.doc
92	More Great Authors (English)	moreauthors_eng.pdf; moreauthors_eng.doc
93	More Great Authors (Spanish)	moreauthors_sp.pdf; moreauthors_sp.doc
94	Great Children's Poets (English)	poets_eng.pdf; poets_eng.doc
95	Great Children's Poets (Spanish)	poets_sp.pdf; poets_sp.doc
96	Reading and Singing (English)	readandsing_eng.pdf; readandsing_eng.doc
97	Reading and Singing (Spanish)	readandsing_sp.pdf; readandsing_sp.doc
98	Things to Remember When Reading to Your Child (English)	remember_eng.pdf; remember_eng.doc
99	Things to Remember When Reading to Your Child (English)	remember_sp.pdf; remember_sp.doc
100	Let's Talk! (English)	letstalk_eng.pdf; letstalk_eng.doc
101	Let's Talk! (Spanish)	letstalk_sp.pdf; letstalk_sp.doc
110	Environmental Print Workshop (English)	ep_eng.pdf; ep_eng.doc
111	Environmental Print Workshop (Spanish)	ep_sp.pdf; ep_sp.doc
112	Environmental Print Workshop: Don't Forget (English)	epdontforget_eng.pdf; epdontforget_eng.doc
113	Environmental Print Workshop: Don't Forget (Spanish)	epdontforget_sp.pdf; epdontforget_sp.doc
114	Environmental Print Workshop Take-Home Letter (English)	eptakehome_eng.pdf; eptakehome_eng.doc
115	Environmental Print Workshop Take-Home Letter (Spanish)	eptakehome_sp.pdf; eptakehome_sp.doc
121	Phonemic Awareness Workshop (English)	pa_eng.pdf; pa_eng.doc
122	Phonemic Awareness Workshop (Spanish)	pa_sp.pdf; pa_sp.doc
123	Phonemic Awareness Workshop: Don't Forget (English)	padontforget_eng.pdf; padontforget_eng.doc
124	Phonemic Awareness Workshop: Don't Forget (Spanish)	padontforget_sp.pdf; padontforget_sp.doc
125	Phonemic Awareness Workshop Take-Home Letter (English)	patakehome_eng.pdf; patakehome_eng.doc
126	Phonemic Awareness Workshop Take-Home Letter (Spanish)	patakehome_sp.pdf; patakehome_sp.doc
131	Read-Aloud Workshop (English)	ra_eng.pdf; ra_eng.doc
132	Read-Aloud Workshop (Spanish)	ra_sp.pdf; ra_sp.doc
133	Read-Aloud Workshop: Don't Forget (English)	radontforget_eng.pdf; radontforget_eng.doc
134	Read-Aloud Workshop: Don't Forget (Spanish)	radontforget_sp.pdf; radontforget_sp.doc
135	Read-Aloud Workshop Take-Home Letter (English)	ratakehome_eng.pdf; ratakehome_eng.doc
136	Read-Aloud Workshop Take-Home Letter (Spanish)	ratakehome_sp.pdf; ratakehome_sp.doc
142	Let's Get Cooking Workshop (English)	lgc_eng.pdf; lgc_eng.doc
143	Let's Get Cooking Workshop (Spanish)	lgc_sp.pdf; lgc_sp.doc
144	Let's Get Cooking Workshop: Don't Forget (English)	lgcdontforget_eng...
145	Let's Get Cooking Workshop: Don't Forget (Spanish)	lgcdo...
146	Let's Get Cooking Workshop Take-Home Letter (English)	l...
147	Let's Get Cooking Workshop Take-Home Letter (Spanish)	
NA	Bonus Art	